# Writing a Behavioral Interve[ntion Plan]
## Based on a
## Functional Behavior Assessment
## Two Day Seminar
## Sixth Edition: FY17

Laura A. Riffel, Ph.D.

C
S          Causal Science Investigator
I

www.behaviordoctor.org

www.twitter.com/behaviordoctor

www.blogtalkradio.com/behaviordoctor

caughtyoubeinggood@gmail.com

# Copyright Page
# ISBN 978-1-365-36641-3

This book is from Behavior Doctor Seminars ®™

Day One Agenda:

8:30-10:00- Ten Tenets of Behavior

10:00-10:15- Break

10:15-11:30- Understanding data collection and then beginning to analyze the data we are collecting

11:30-12:45- Lunch

12:45- 2:00- Data Analysis

2:00-2:15- Break

2:15-3:30- Data Analysis, Data Collection Tools, Synthesis and Evaluation

Day Two Agenda:

8:30-10:00- Data entry for Ralph Cunningham Data

10:00-10:15- Break

10:15-11:30- Writing a BIP for Ralph Cunningham based on Data Entry- Collecting Intervention Data

11:30-12:45- Lunch

12:45-2:00- Other data collection tools and techniques (When to use what data collection tool)

2:00-2:15- Break

2:15-3:30- Triple T- Triple R examples

Learning Objectives:

Participants who attend this training will learn the ten tenets of behavior. Understanding the tenets will help us understand where and why behavior appears in the classroom. All behavior is communication. Afterwards, participants will be able to take ten days of real data, plug it into an analysis tool, discuss with table mates and learn the functions and triggers of behavior. After analysis of Scout's data, the participants will learn how to plug this into the Triple T-Triple R Chart to build a behavioral intervention plan that is data-based decision making. This is the ABC's of behavior in a simplified version. Participants will leave with an understanding of FBA and BIP. Participants will also learn how to enter data into a free FBA Data Tool and use that information to write a data-based quality BIP.

www.behaviordoctor.org

Laura A. Riffel, Ph.D.

caughtyoubeinggood@gmail.com

It was developed to be used in conjunction with a seminar on Functional Behavior Assessment

# Writing a Behavioral Intervention Plan (BIP) based on a Functional Behavior Assessment (FBA)

**Ten Tenets of Behavior:**

1. Behavior is learned and serves a specific purpose (Bandura)
2. Behavior is related to the context within which it occurs (Bambara & Knoster)
3. For every year a behavior has been in place, we need to expect one month of consistent and appropriate intervention to see a change (Atchison)
4. We can improve behavior by 80% just by pointing out what one person is doing correctly (Shores, Gunter, Jack)
5. We use positive behavior specific praise about 6.25% of the time (Haydon, et al.)
6. When we want compliance in our students we should whisper in their right ear (Live Science)
7. All behavior has function and falls into two categories: To gain access to or to Escape from (Alberto & Troutman)
8. To Gain Access- see chart on page 4
9. To Escape From- see chart on page 4
10. Your reaction determines whether a behavior will occur again. We have to change our behavior (Alberto & Troutman).

First things first, we should probably define what we mean by function of behavior. The function is the end result that maintains the behavior. It is the reason a behavior occurs in most cases. Function is broken into two main categories:

**Functions of Behavior**

| To Gain | To Escape |
|---|---|
| Attention: | Work/Tasks/chores |
| • Peers | People |
| • Adults | • Adults |
| Access to preferred items or environmental controls | • Peers (Think bullying) |
| | Pain |
| Sensory Integration (Input) | • Emotional |
| | • Physical |
| | Sensory (Overload) |

## Multi-modal plans:

We need to create a plan that is not based on just one intervention. It has to be effective. We need to manage consequences to reinforce the desired behaviors and replacement skills we teach to the student. We need to withhold reinforcement following the target behavior. We need to use natural and least intrusive consequences that will address the function of the behavior.

## Triggers that Set Behavior in Motion

### Setting Events or Contexts

Setting events are things that happened in the near distant past. Most likely, the educator did not see these things occur. There are many different setting events that play into behavior. What did you brainstorm in your group?

### Antecedents

Another word we need to define is antecedent. An antecedent is anything that occurs prior to the exhibition of the behavior. This might occur right before the behavior, but it can also be a slow trigger that occurs earlier in the day and manifests later. Antecedents can be contexts, settings, situations or conditions. Here is a simple list of common antecedents:

| Transition | Frustration | Denied access | Task demand | Presence of a certain peer or adult |
|---|---|---|---|---|
| Time of day | Day of week | Perceived attention | Proximity | Noises |
| Smells | Subjects | Activities | Changes in schedule | Emotional upset |

Unfortunately, children do not wear signs that announce they are experiencing many of these things. The behavior support team must meet prior to collecting data and they must discuss which of these may be triggers and then define what that looks like for that particular child. Including the parent on the behavior support team is imperative because they can be an integral member alerting the staff to lack of sleep, not feeling well, or emotional upset that might be occurring.

### Behavior

Frequently, when we are asked to assist with behavior change the staff tell us the behaviors they want to target for change and they have a list of eight different behaviors for one child. While we don't deny some children have eight behaviors in one day, it is impossible to measure eight behaviors and still teach. We feel it is extremely important for the classroom teacher to be the one collecting data, so we focus on one behavior at a time. We start with the behavior of highest need or highest rate. We take care of that behavior and then what happens is many other little behaviors disappear. We then take on the next biggest behavior.

We need to define the behavior in measurable and observable terms. We frequently hear things like this:

- Poor impulse control
- Angry, hostile, and resentful
- Not Paying Attention
- Stubborn

We all have a different definition for each one of these depending upon our mood or circumstance. We have to label the behaviors in a way that anyone collecting data in the room or if eight teachers are collecting data throughout the day, we will all measure it the same way. Here are some better examples:

- Lying on the floor and refusing to move
- High pitched screams
- Hitting with fist
- Kicking over chairs
- Not beginning work within five minutes of task demand

Many times a child is engaging in tantrum behavior and the team will write tantrum. Once again, what one person calls a tantrum another person might just call letting off steam. If we are determining the function of a tantrum, we need to define it by very concrete measures. Here is an example:

- A tantrum includes at least three of the following behaviors occurring in conjunction with each other:
    - Lying on the floor and refusing to move
    - Screaming loudly
    - Throwing objects
    - Hitting with fists
    - Cursing
    - Self-injurious behavior such as banging head on the floor

This makes the definition clearer for anyone to identify a real tantrum from a little fit.

### impacT (What are they gaining or escaping)

## Consequence

The next term we need to define is consequence. Typically, people think of punishment when they hear the word consequence. When we are thinking of consequences in terms of function of behavior, we are thinking about what specifically is maintaining the behavior. Think of it this way, your paycheck is a consequence of working. Having this paycheck is the consequence that keeps you coming to work each day. I'm sure there are a few of us who would work for free, but for the most part, we are going for the paycheck because we need it to live.

The consequence is determined by the function. We have to ask ourselves what the child is trying to get or what they are trying to avoid by having the behavior. We can guess all we want, but until we collect the data all we are doing is guessing. We did an experiment in 2004. We served 100 students with autism that year. Every referral that came in to the office, we had the main referrer fill out a Problem Behavior Questionnaire (PBQ). We scored the PBQ and then put it in a file sealed from the behavior specialist. The team then conducted a full FBA on the student, put an intervention in place based on the function found in the FBA and kept the intervention going until there was an 80% or better decrease from baseline. A few tweaks were typically made in the intervention; however, the function of the behavior always remained the same from the full FBA. After the case was closed by the behavior specialist, we pulled out the PBQ and compared the function on the PBQ (which is someone's opinion). The reliability measure on the PBQ was 28%. This means the function determined from the PBQ or the person's opinion of the behavior was only right 3 out of 10 times. If we put the wrong intervention in place and we are not feeding the correct function, often the behavior exacerbates. In many cases a full FBA is necessary to determine the real consequences feeding the behavior.

**Behavior Support Team**

The Behavior Support Team (BST) is the next term we need to define. The BST should include the following people:

- Parents
- Teachers involved with the student
- Educator with behavioral expertise
- An administrative designee

Also, the team might include any of the following people:

- Student themselves
- Therapists
- Community support (social workers, probation officers, after school care)
- Transportation provider
- Relatives
- Support teachers

This team should be filled with people who genuinely are interested in a positive outcome for the student. We have found more than 14 people in a room is counterproductive to finding results. Often when there are more than 14 people, the focus is on admiring the problem rather than finding a solution.

**Steps for the First BST**

**Strengths**

The BST should meet before any data are collected. The first step of the BST is to focus on the student's strengths and needs. We prefer the strengths are posted on a large poster, white board or smart board and they are left up throughout the process. Here is a guide:

**Skylar's Strengths:**

| Social Strengths | Academic Strengths |
| --- | --- |
| Friendly | Begins work right away |
| Never absent | Nice handwriting |
| Nice smile | Brings back homework |
| Supportive family | Asks questions when unclear |

We like to have blank forms lying on the table when everyone walks in the room. It is also important to let everyone know the first thing you will be talking about are the student's strengths. Be sure to call the parents and have them bring a list of things they know their child is good at performing. One person should be the recorder for the BST and they should write everyone's ideas on the Smartboard, whiteboard, or poster. Make sure all of these are positive before they are written down.

**Needs**

The next step is to discuss needs. What does the student need? These can still be framed positively if you focus on what the staff need to provide, not what the student needs to do.

| Social Needs | Academic Needs |
| --- | --- |
| Help in keeping friendships | Help in comprehension for reading skills |
| Help in keeping negative opinions to himself | Help in calculations for multiplication skills at the two digit by two-digit level |
| Help in taking constructive feedback | Help in writing a paragraph that stays on topic |
| Help in inviting friends over to his house to play | Help in transitioning quietly from one subject to the next |

These strengths will help guide the team for antecedent modifications once the data are collected.

**Behaviors to Target**

The next step is to focus on target behavior. While there may be more than one behavior, it is a good idea to limit the target to the one the team thinks is the most disruptive to learning. This behavior should be defined in measurable and observable terms and written down for everyone. When we say "blurting", this is what we mean: "The teacher asks for a response and tells the students to raise their hand and Skylar blurts out the answer before anyone gets a chance to be called on; or, Skylar blurts out negative comments when other students answer the question for the teacher."

## Data Collection

The next step is to determine with the team who is going to collect data, what data they will collect and how long they will collect the data. There are many different ways to collect data.

Indirect method

- Anecdotal notes
- Surveys
- Interviews

Direct method

- Observational
- Data collection
    - ABC Data Collection
    - Minute by Minute Data
    - Frequency Data
    - Duration Data
    - Scatter Plot
    - Interval Time Sample

## How Much Data Should You Collect?

We used to require ten days of data collection. We realize this is a lot of data to expect and no one ever said ten days was imperative. Here is the rationale: if a student is affected by certain days of the week, then we want to have two examples of each day of the week. Just one example of a day of the week might be an outlier. If we collect ten days of data, and one Monday has 34 behaviors and the next Monday has three behaviors, we can collect one more Monday of data to determine which day is the truth and which day is an outlier. If this is too daunting of a task, then at least ten incidents of the behavior must be collected. Some students provide these ten incidents in ten minutes. We do not recommend a ten-minute data collection. Please collect at least three to five days of data to determine the best function. The more data you collect the better you will be able to see the patterns.

## Which Data Form Will You Use?

**High Frequency Behaviors.** Suppose you have a student who interrupts the teacher 63 times in 30 minutes. You would not want to collect data on antecedents, behaviors, and consequences for each behavior. You will want to do a frequency count or an interval time sample and use anecdotal notes to determine the triggers and consequences of the behavior. A minute-by-minute sheet might be an effective tool which can be matched to the student's schedule along with anecdotal note

**Low Frequency Behaviors.** Sometimes a behavior occurs so infrequently, but is such high intensity it is imperative to determine the function of the behavior. Here's an example: an adult with autism, bi-polar condition, intellectual disabilities, and mild cerebral palsy would miss work for two or three days every five to seven weeks. There did not seem to be a pattern to this behavior, but he would refuse to eat, drink, or take his medication. He did not go to the restroom either. After 24 hours, he had to be hospitalized for fluids and medications. This was distressing to him and to his family. We took a year's worth of data and observed it for patterns. We laid it out on the table and tried to match it to things like: moon cycle, parents being in town, caregivers being in town, sisters being in town and so on. There did not seem to be a pattern. After staring at the data for some time, the team went over to the weather department and asked them to run the barometric pressure for one year looking at day 1's barometric pressure average and comparing it to day 2 and so on from day to day. Barometric pressure is measured in inches so one day it might be 28.32 and the next day it might be 27.45. We had no idea if anything would pan out, but it seemed like the only other idea we had at the time. When we laid out the data, we found if there was a certain inch change in the barometric pressure from day to day then the adult client would start a downward spiral in his lock-down behavior. Please don't take from this that it has to do with barometric pressure for every child or that it even has to do with a certain inch change in barometric pressure. We worked with a seven-year-old child with Asperger syndrome and bi-polar condition and he was manic on high barometric pressure days and depressed on low barometric pressure days and if the barometric pressure stayed pretty even for several days, he stayed pretty even keel for those days. What we think is that it is as individualized as the children we work with on a daily basis.

**Disruptive Behaviors.** For most disruptive behaviors, you will want to collect antecedent, behavior and consequence data using the ABC form. You will be taught how to use the FBA Data Tool from Behavior Doctor Seminars in this training.

**Aggressive Behaviors.** If someone is getting hurt either themselves or others, then a crisis plan needs to be put in place prior to any data collection.

Samples of all the data tools begin on page 31.

**Let's Do a Sample and Then We Will Come Back to Learning More**

# Meet Scout Radley

## Strengths and Needs

| Social Strengths | Academic Strengths | Social Needs | Academic Needs |
|---|---|---|---|
| • Comfortable talking in front of the whole class<br>• Great supportive family<br>• Vocabulary is advanced for her age | • Scout is very visual and can draw pictures better than anyone in the class<br>• Scout always turns in her work<br>• Scout has neat cursive handwriting | • Scout is very comfortable with adults but needs to make friends with peers<br>• Scout needs help with transitions<br>• Scout needs to keep hands and feet to self | • Scout needs help with reading comprehension<br>• Scout needs help with reading fluency<br>• Scout needs help in learning to ask for help |

Scout is a sixth grade student in a K-6 grade school. She is with the same teacher all day and in a class of 25 students. The school has 476 students and is a neighborhood school. She has not been retained and is a "young" student in the class compared to her peers. Her older sisters are both in high school and are very athletic and popular with many friends. Scout tends to hang out with the sisters' friends and rarely has friends her own age over to the house.

She has mild learning difficulties. Scout has two siblings who attend the nearby high school. Scout's mother works full time and father frequently travels. He leaves on Sunday evening and returns on Friday afternoon.

Scout's behaviors at school are disruptive outbursts, physical aggression, and throwing objects. When we got to the school and observed, we changed physical aggression to horseplay. They insisted on calling it physical aggression. It was the Volkswagen Slug Bug Tap that your kids do in the back seat of the car when they see a Volkswagen. We would call that horseplay. You will see we changed their category when we set up the data for your training.

Mom reports Scout is disorganized at home and leaves her stuff laying all over the house. Mom says she is so disorganized they have three or four fights every morning. She says she has to drive Scout to school because she would make the whole bus late if they waited on Scout. Mom says Scout eats everything in sight when she gets home from school and fights with her sisters until her Mom gets home in the evening.

Scout is included in the regular classroom with support provided by a co-teaching special education teacher who works with the regular classroom teacher.

## Behaviors

We defined Scouts behaviors as follows:

| Throwing objects means a physical object leaves Scout's hands with purpose and lands at least 12 inches from her body | Disruptive outburst means a loud verbal sound or word that comes from Scout and disturbs the learning environment | Horseplay was the Volkswagen slug bug tap that kids do to each other in the back seat of the car. Knuckle out and into someone's arm. |

## Data

We brainstormed as a team the possible context/setting events, antecedents, behaviors, consequences, and student responses. Here is Scout's list generated by the team.

| Start Time | End Time | Context/ Setting Event | | Antecedent | | Behavior | | Consequence | | Student Response | |
|---|---|---|---|---|---|---|---|---|---|---|---|
| | | A | Group Time | A | Transition | A | Throwing Objects | A | Consequences | A | Group Time |
| | | B | Individual Work | B | Choice given | B | Disruptive Outburst | B | Choice given | B | Individual Work |
| | | C | Reading | C | Redirection | C | Horseplay | C | Redirection | C | Reading |
| | | D | Math | D | Instruction directive | | | D | Discussion | D | Math |
| | | E | Spelling | E | New task | | | E | Personal space given | E | Spelling |
| | | F | Social Studies | F | Routine task | | | F | Changed activity | F | Social Studies |
| | | G | Science | G | Physical prompts | | | G | Peer attention | G | Science |
| | | H | Free Choice | H | Teacher attention to others | | | H | Verbal reprimand | H | Free Choice |
| | | I | Lunch | I | Told "NO" | | | I | Physical prompt | I | Lunch |
| | | J | Outside | J | Close proximity | | | J | Time out | J | Outside |
| | | K | | K | Interaction with others | | | | | K | |

The team then collected data for ten days. Anyone who worked with Scout collected data for the time she was in their view. All of this data was then compiled for a true picture of Scout's days.

Name: _____ Person filling out: _____

Data Collection Form:  Date: _____ Day of the Week: _____

| Start Time | End Time | Context/ Setting Event | | Antecedent | | Behavior | | Consequence | | Student Response | |
|---|---|---|---|---|---|---|---|---|---|---|---|
| | | A | Group Time | A | Transition | A | Throwing Objects | A | Consequences | A | Stopped |
| | | B | Individual Work | B | Choice given | B | Disruptive Outburst | B | Choice given | B | Continued |
| | | C | Reading | C | Redirection | C | Horseplay | C | Redirection | C | Intensified |
| | | D | Math | D | Instruction directive | | | D | Discussion | | |
| | | E | Spelling | E | New task | | | E | Personal space given | | |
| | | F | Social Studies | F | Routine task | | | F | Changed activity | | |
| | | G | Science | G | Physical prompts | | | G | Peer attention | | |
| | | H | Free Choice | H | Teacher attention to others | | | H | Verbal reprimand | | |
| | | I | Lunch | I | Told "NO" | | | I | Physical prompt | | |
| | | J | Outside | J | Close proximity | | | J | Time out | | |
| | | K | | K | Interaction with others | | | | | | |

| Start Time | End Time | Context Setting Event | Antecedent | Behavior | Consequence | Reaction |
|---|---|---|---|---|---|---|
| | | | | | | |
| | | | | | | |
| | | | | | | |
| | | | | | | |
| | | | | | | |
| | | | | | | |
| | | | | | | |
| | | | | | | |
| | | | | | | |
| | | | | | | |
| | | | | | | |
| | | | | | | |
| | | | | | | |
| | | | | | | |
| | | | | | | |
| | | | | | | |
| | | | | | | |
| | | | | | | |
| | | | | | | |
| | | | | | | |

Writing Behavioral Intervention Plans       Laura A. Riffel, Ph.D.

So here are Scout's 10 days of Data:

Readers- you will read letters to recorders from these next forms.

May 1, 2014 Thursday

| Time Start | Time End | Context (Setting) | Antecedent | Behavior | Consequence | Student Behavior |
|---|---|---|---|---|---|---|
| 8:30 | 8:59 | A | A | B | B | B |
| 9:20 | 9:22 | C | E | C | I | A |
| 12:15 | 12:17 | I | H | A | C | A |
| 3:05 | 3:30 | A | A | B | B | B |

May 2, 2014 Friday

| Time Start | Time End | Context (Setting) | Antecedent | Behavior | Consequence | Student Behavior |
|---|---|---|---|---|---|---|
| 8:32 | 8:34 | A | A | B | B | A |
| 9:10 | 9:11 | C | D | C | I | A |
| 12:12 | 12:17 | I | H | A | F | B |
| 2:55 | 3:30 | A | A | B | C | C |

May 5, 2014 Monday

| Time Start | Time End | Context (Setting) | Antecedent | Behavior | Consequence | Student Behavior |
|---|---|---|---|---|---|---|
| 8:40 | 8:46 | A | A | B | E | B |
| 9:17 | 9:40 | C | E | C | I | C |
| 12:30 | 12:32 | I | H | B | A | A |
| 1:15 | 1:17 | D | E | B | A | A |
| 3:00 | 3:30 | A | A | B | C | B |

May 6, 2014 Tuesday

| Time Start | Time End | Context (Setting) | Antecedent | Behavior | Consequence | Student Behavior |
|---|---|---|---|---|---|---|
| 8:30 | 8:42 | A | A | B | E | B |
| 3:10 | 3:12 | A | A | B | B | A |
|  |  |  |  |  |  |  |

May 7, 2014 Wednesday

| Time Start | Time End | Context (Setting) | Antecedent | Behavior | Consequence | Student Behavior |
|---|---|---|---|---|---|---|
| 12:15 | 12:30 | I | H | B | B | B |
|  |  |  |  |  |  |  |
|  |  |  |  |  |  |  |

May 8, 2014 Thursday

| Time Start | Time End | Context (Setting) | Antecedent | Behavior | Consequence | Student Behavior |
|---|---|---|---|---|---|---|
| 9:15 | 9:48 | C | E | C | I | C |
| 3:15 | 3:17 | A | A | B | A | A |
|  |  |  |  |  |  |  |

May 9, 2014 Friday

| Time Start | Time End | Context (Setting) | Antecedent | Behavior | Consequence | Student Behavior |
|---|---|---|---|---|---|---|
| 8:30 | 8:32 | A | A | B | C | A |
| 12:10 | 12:12 | I | H | B | A | A |
| 1:15 | 1:32 | D | E | C | I | B |
| 2:20 | 2:45 | E | D | C | I | B |
| 3:01 | 3:30 | A | A | B | B | B |

May 12, 2014 Monday

| Time Start | Time End | Context (Setting) | Antecedent | Behavior | Consequence | Student Behavior |
|---|---|---|---|---|---|---|
| 8:30 | 8:42 | A | A | B | A | B |
| 9:15 | 9:17 | C | E | C | I | A |
| 10:15 | 10:17 | D | H | B | B | A |
| 12:07 | 12:22 | I | H | B | F | B |
| 1:15 | 1:17 | D | E | C | I | A |
| 3:10 | 3:30 | A | A | B | B | B |

May 13, 2014 Tuesday

| Time Start | Time End | Context (Setting) | Antecedent | Behavior | Consequence | Student Behavior |
|---|---|---|---|---|---|---|
| 9:17 | 9:19 | C | D | C | I | A |
|  |  |  |  |  |  |  |

May 14, 2014 Wednesday

| Time Start | Time End | Context (Setting) | Antecedent | Behavior | Consequence | Student Behavior |
|---|---|---|---|---|---|---|
| 1:15 | 1:32 | D | E | C | I | B |
| 3:15 | 3:17 | A | A | B | A | A |
|  |  |  |  |  |  |  |
|  |  |  |  |  |  |  |
|  |  |  |  |  |  |  |

Please pair up with a small group and tabulate the data:

A. Total Days of Data: _____

B. Total Incidents: _____

C. Average per day (b/a) _____

D. Total number of minutes engaged in target behavior _____379 minutes_____

E. Average length of time for each behavior (D/B) _____

F. Percent of Day (D/total minutes for entire data collection) (420 minutes per day x 10 days)

_____

Time of Day:

|  | Go through all ten days of data and tally once for when the behavior started- not how long it lasted. For instance: the behavior might have started at 8:49 and lasted till 9:15- but you would only make a tally in the 8:30-8:59 row. We are looking for trigger times. What time does behavior start? |
|---|---|
| 8:30-8:59 |  |
| 9:00-9:29 |  |
| 9:30-9:59 |  |
| 10:00-10:29 |  |
| 10:30-10:59 |  |
| 11:00-11:29 |  |
| 11:30-11:59 |  |
| 12:00-12:29 |  |
| 12:30-12:59 |  |
| 1:00-1:29 |  |
| 1:30-1:59 |  |
| 2:00-2:29 |  |
| 2:30-2:59 |  |
| 3:00-3:30 |  |

Day of the Week

|  | Go through the ten days and add the two Mondays together and divide by two for an average- then complete all the days of the week in the same fashion. |
|---|---|
| Monday |  |
| Tuesday |  |
| Wednesday |  |
| Thursday |  |
| Friday |  |

Now tally the contexts:

| CONTEXT | LETTER | TALLY | RATIO | PERCENT |
|---|---|---|---|---|
| Group time | A |  |  |  |
| Individual time | B |  |  |  |
| Reading | C |  |  |  |
| Math | D |  |  |  |
| Spelling | E |  |  |  |
| Social studies | F |  |  |  |
| Science | G |  |  |  |
| Home room | H |  |  |  |
| Lunch | I |  |  |  |
| Outside | J |  |  |  |

Tally the behaviors just to see if we have enough data and which behavior she is most likely to engage:

| Behavior | letter | Tallies of each incident | Ratio of Total | Percent of Engagement |
|---|---|---|---|---|
| Throwing Objects | A | | | |
| Disruptive Outburst | B | | | |
| Horseplay | C | | | |

Next tally the antecedents:

| ANTECEDENTS | LETTER | TALLY | RATIO | PERCENT |
|---|---|---|---|---|
| Transition | A | | | |
| Choice given | B | | | |
| Redirection | C | | | |
| Instruction directive | D | | | |
| New task | E | | | |
| Routine task | F | | | |
| Physical prompts | G | | | |
| Teacher attention to others | H | | | |
| Told "NO" | I | | | |
| Close proximity | J | | | |
| Interaction with others | K | | | |

Now we will look at antecedents paired with each behavior:

| ANTECEDENTS | LETTER | Throwing objects  A | Disruptive outbursts  B | Horseplay  C |
|---|---|---|---|---|
| Transition | A | | | |
| Choice given | B | | | |
| Redirection | C | | | |
| Instruction directive | D | | | |
| New task | E | | | |
| Routine task | F | | | |
| Physical prompts | G | | | |
| Teacher attention to others | H | | | |
| Told "NO" | I | | | |
| Close proximity | J | | | |
| Interaction with others | K | | | |

Next we will do the same thing with consequences:

| Consequences | LETTER | Throwing objects  A | Disruptive outbursts  B | Horseplay  C |
|---|---|---|---|---|
| Choice given | A | | | |
| Redirection | B | | | |
| Discussion | C | | | |
| Personal space given | D | | | |
| Changed activity | E | | | |
| Peer attention | F | | | |
| Verbal reprimand | G | | | |
| Physical prompt | H | | | |
| Time out | I | | | |

What patterns did you see for time of day?

**FREQUENCY OF BEHAVIORS** Each bar in the graph below represents the number of behaviors observed in each 30 minute time segment during this assessment period.

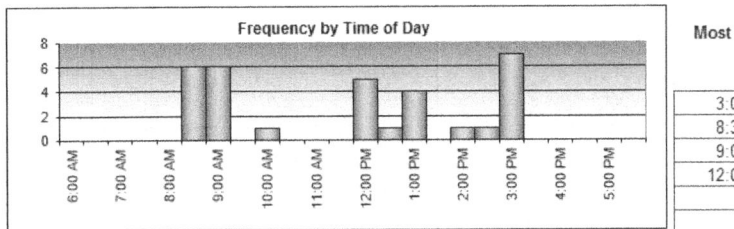

What patterns did you see for day of week data?

Writing Behavioral Intervention Plans    Laura A. Riffel, Ph.D.

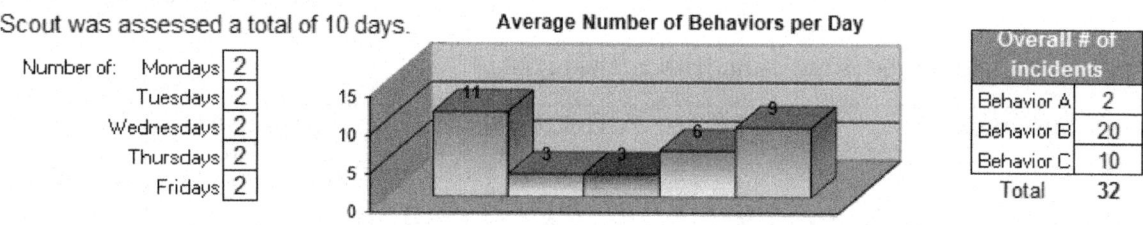

What patterns did you see for which behaviors she used?

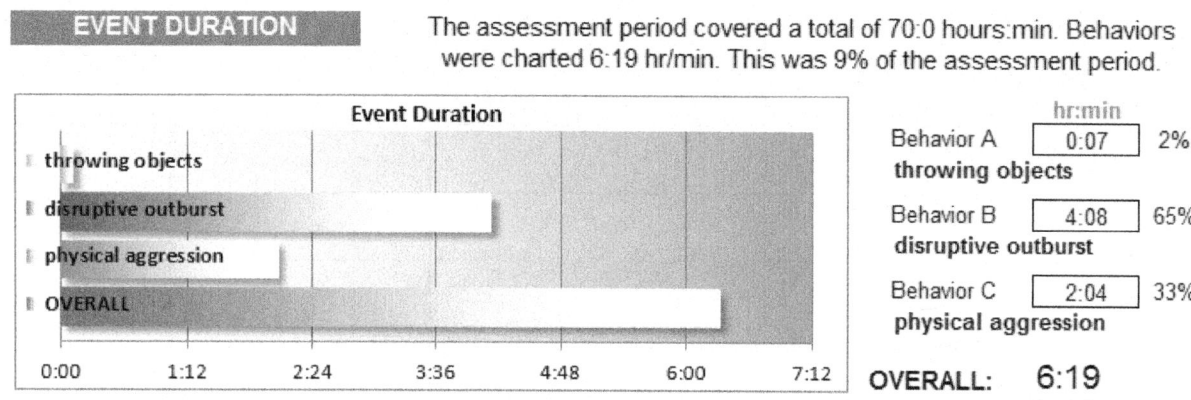

What patterns did you see for contexts paired with behaviors?

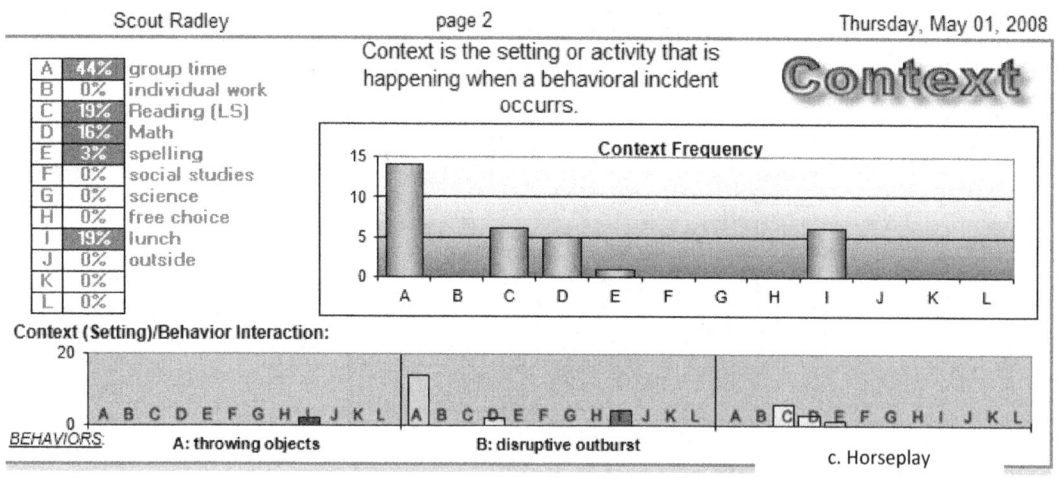

What patterns did you see for antecedents paired with behaviors?

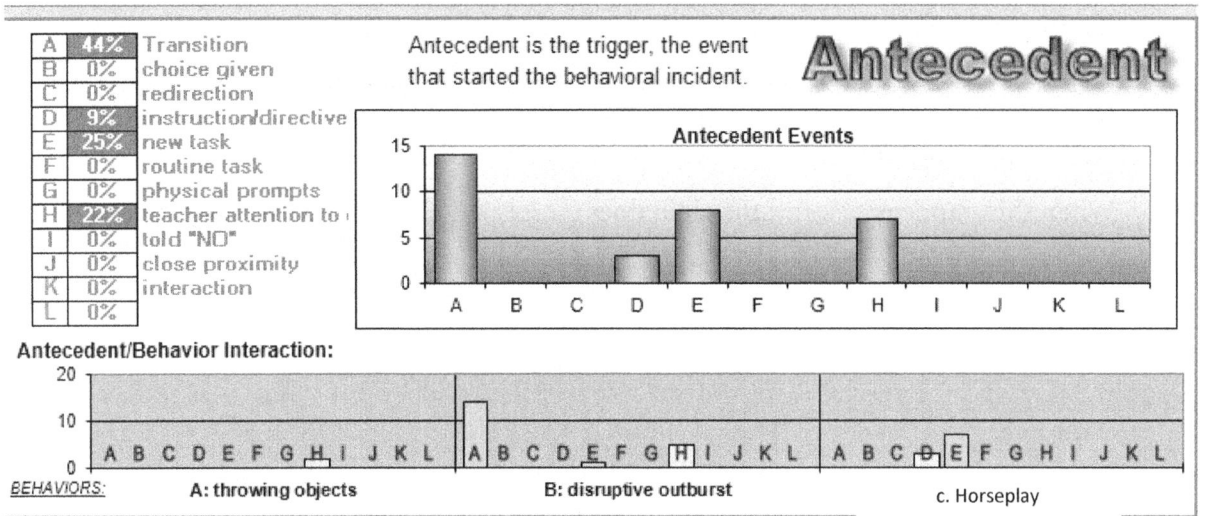

What patterns did you see for consequences paired with behaviors?

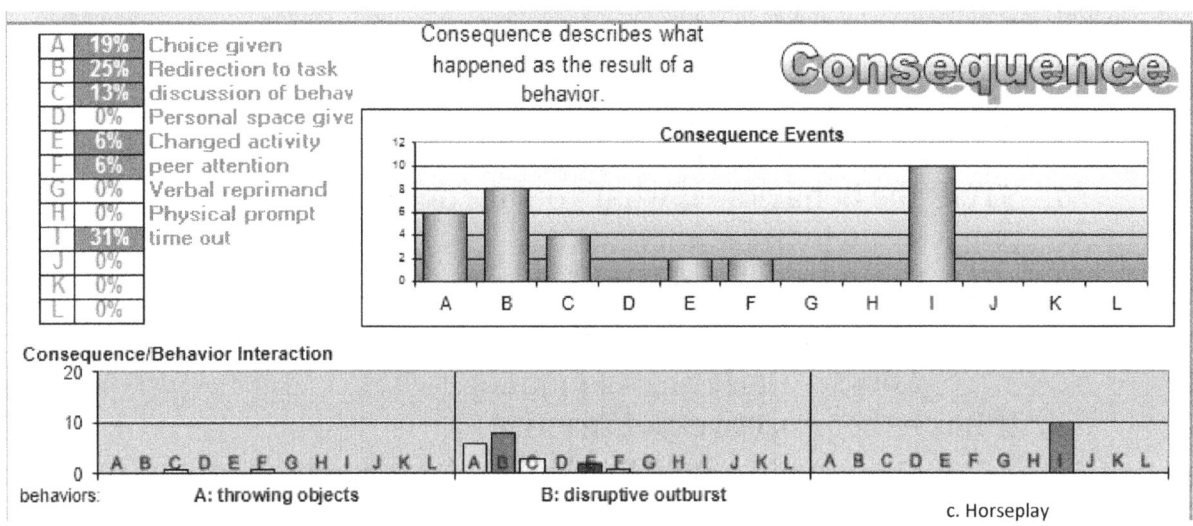

Summary Statements:

Our next task is to determine a summary statement for each function. Since Scout has two functions, we need to have three different summary statements. A summary statement is the foundation for building the intervention plan.

When this happens……………the child does ………………………… to (get or get out) of ………………….

When Scout has _____, Scout has a disruptive outburst, to _____.

When Scout has _____, Scout engages in horseplay, to _____.

Golden Nugget:

To be a real intervention it has to do the following:
1. STOP the behavior- if what you are doing does not stop the behavior- why repeat it?
   a. Example- if a student has been to the office 47 times- what makes us think the 48th time will be the time it works?
2. It has to be proactive-not reactive
   a. Reacting to a behavior will not change it once it has been taught
   b. Remember "behavior is learned"
3. It has to include environmental changes where you set the student up to be successful
   a. It has to be more fun to engage in the right behavior than it is to engage in the targeted behavior
4. It has to include replacement behavior teaching- you can't just say "stop burping"- you have to tell them what to do instead
5. It has to include changes to your own behavior- because your behavior is feeding their behavior.

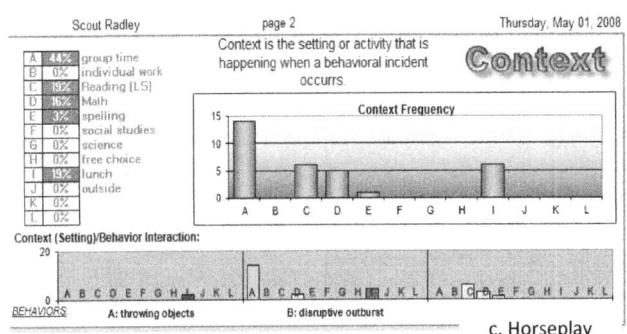
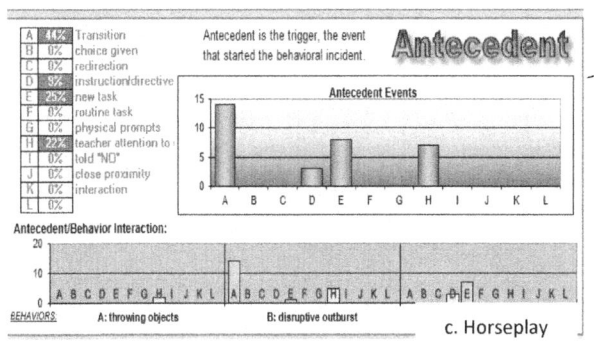

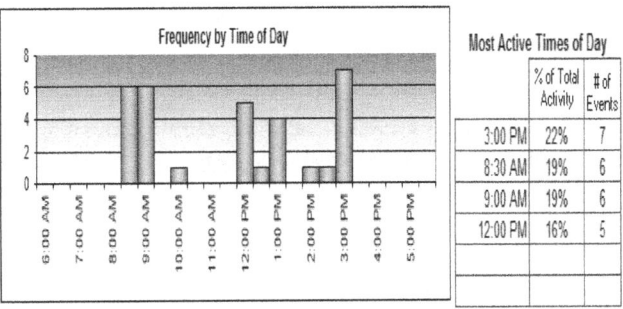
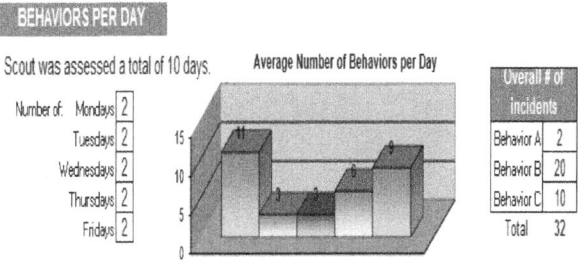

| Trigger | Target | impacT |
|---|---|---|
|  | **Disruptive Outburst** |  |
|  | **Horseplay** |  |

What patterns do you see from the data above that might be triggers for each of the two behaviors we are focusing on? (Disruptive Outbursts and Horseplay)

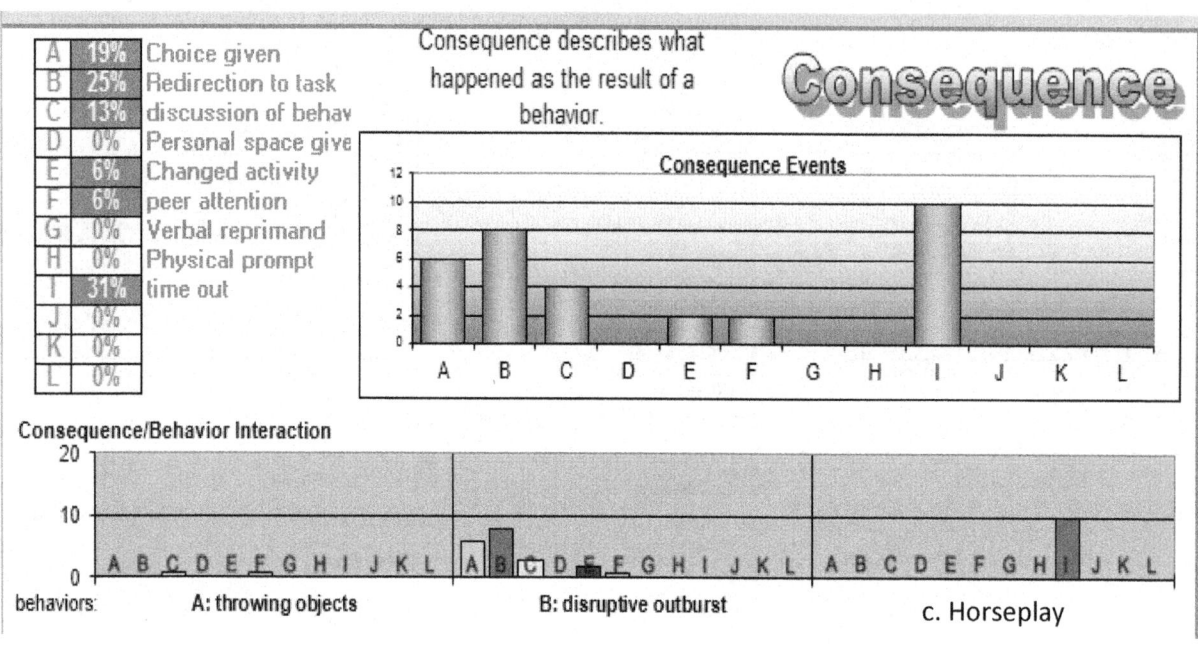

| Trigger | Target | impacT |
|---|---|---|
|  | **Disruptive Outburst** |  |
|  | **Horseplay** |  |

What impacT do you see from the data above that might be feeding the two behaviors we are focusing on? (Disruptive Outburst and Horseplay)

We have revamped the competing pathway chart. It seemed to confuse many people. We are calling this the Triple "T" chart. Our summary statement is made up of the "Trigger-Target- impacT". These are the items on either side of the behavior that feed it.

Once we know the summary statement, we can build a plan based on factual data and not our opinion. We call this the Triple "R" chart.

| Trigger | Target | impacT |
|---|---|---|
| When there is a transition paired with group time | Scout has a Disruptive Outburst | To get adult attention. |
| **Revise the Environment** | **Replace the Behavior** | **Reframe the Response** |
|  |  |  |

Writing Behavioral Intervention Plans     Laura A. Riffel, Ph.D.

| Trigger | Target | impacT |
|---|---|---|
| When there is a new task that involves reading | Scout engages in horseplay | To get escape work. |
| **Revise the Environment** | **Replace the Behavior** | **Reframe the Response** |
| | | |

**Baseline to Intervention:**

To determine the baseline, we take the data from the functional behavior assessment data and then we put the intervention in place and take probe data (just frequency or duration) and compare it to the baseline data.

Scout's data points for baseline and intervention look like this:

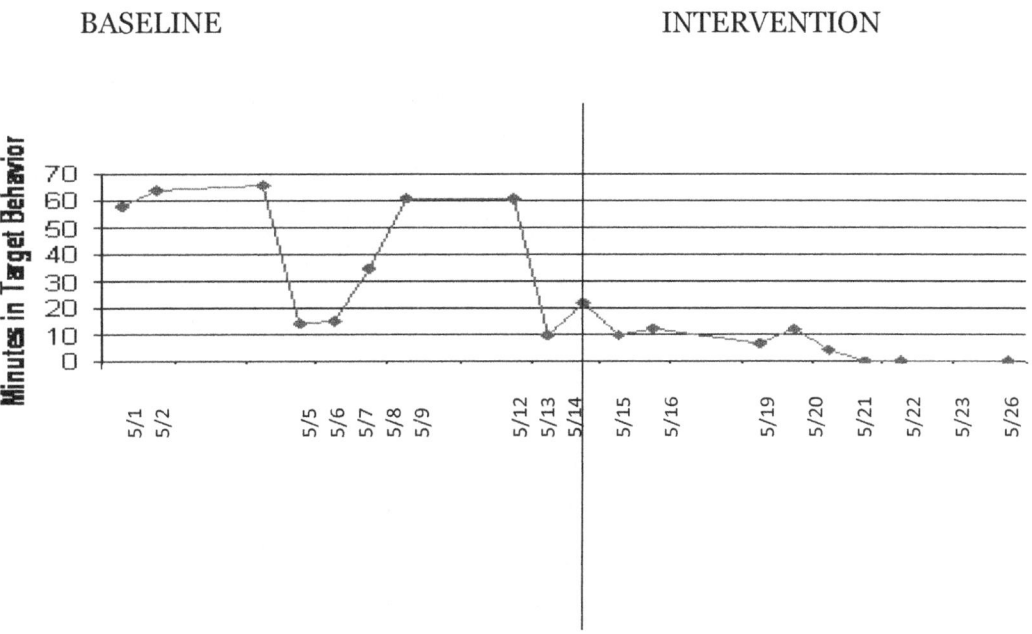

You do not need to collect full FBA data after the initial data set produces the appropriate amount of data for developing a BIP.

**Formula for determining decrease from baseline:**

(I-B)/B=D*100

Intervention Data= "I" – Baseline Data= "B" and Decrease = "D"

Intervention Frequency = 3 times per day

Baseline Frequency = 34 times per day

3-34= -31

-31/34= -.91176

-91 x 100=

**-91% Decrease from Baseline**

**Day Two**
**Entering Data**

# Ralph Cunningham

## Data Collected Over Ten Days

First, open your FBA data tool that you downloaded this morning.

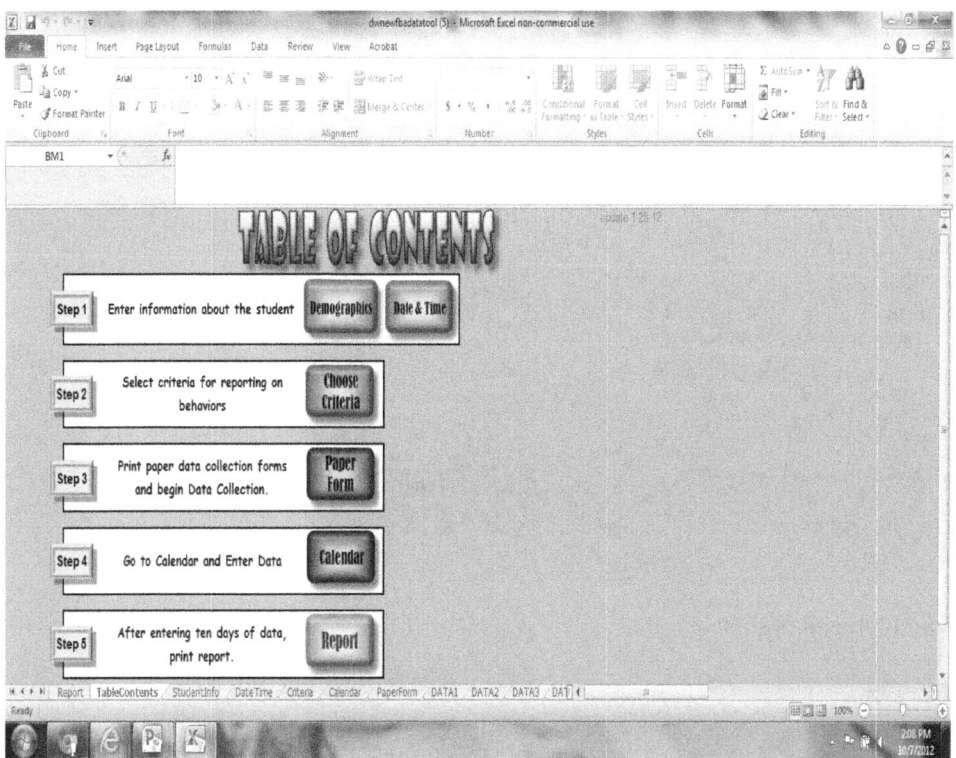

Click demographics and enter information

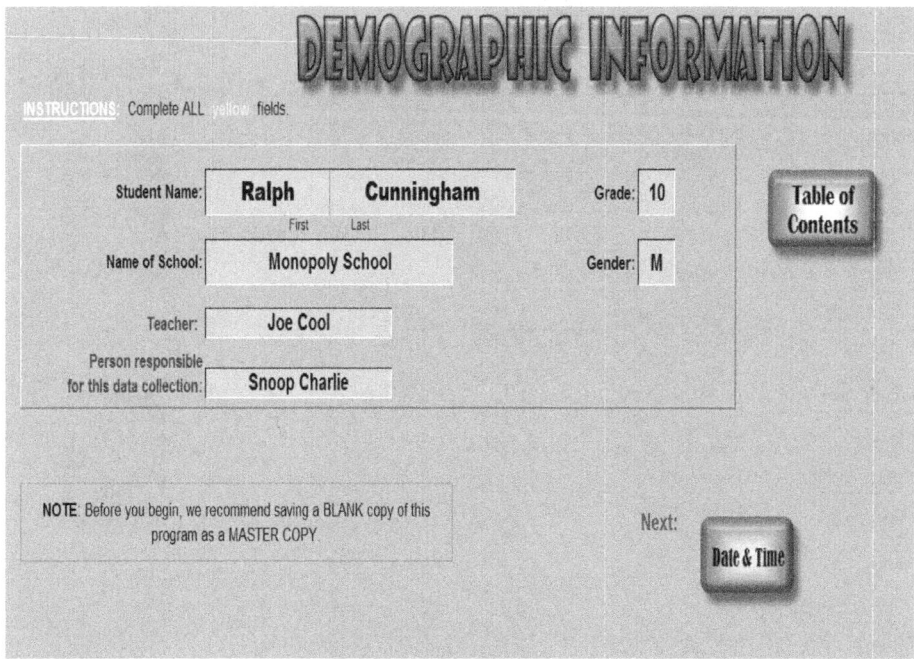

Click Date and Time

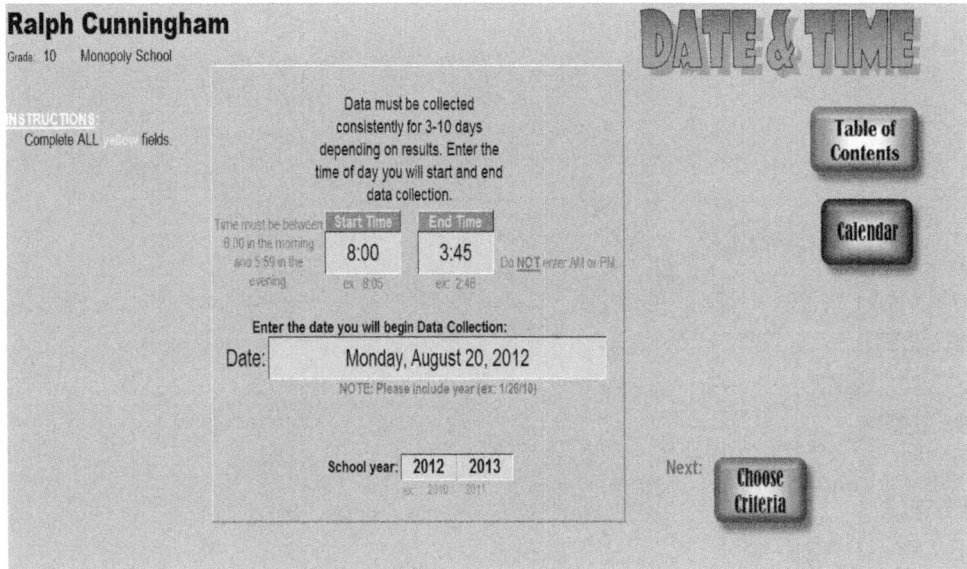

Click choose criteria and type all of this

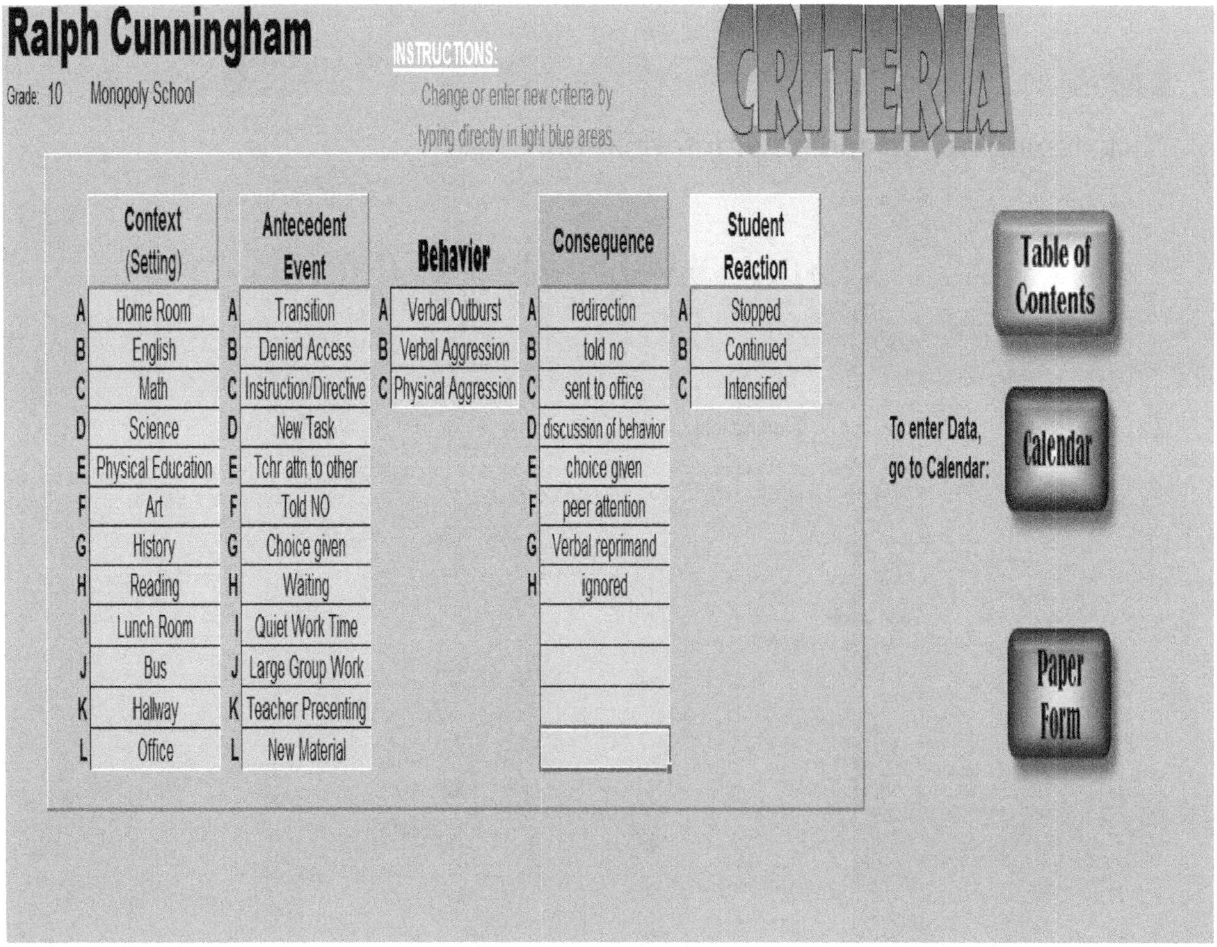

Now you will enter the data into the calendar

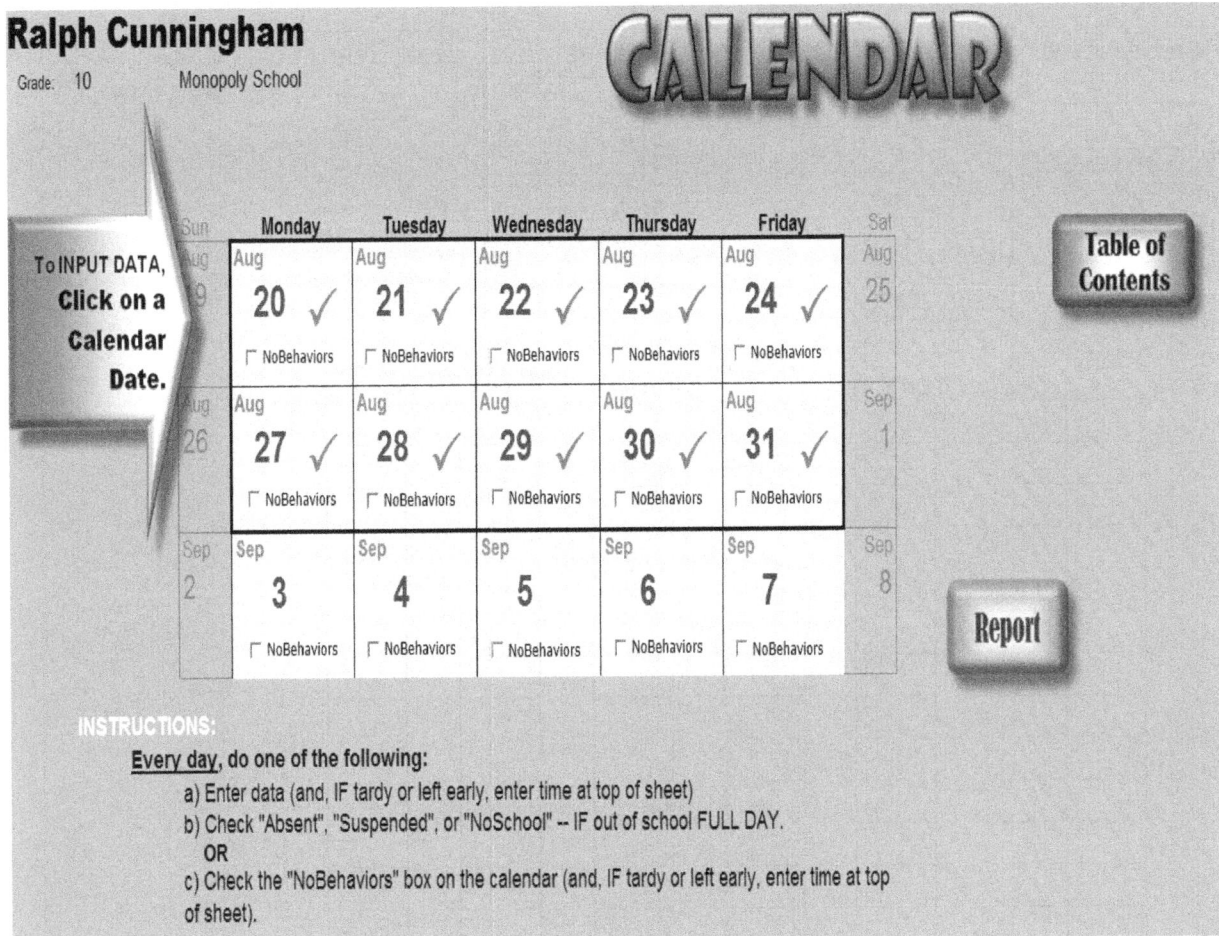

Click August 20th and start entering the data on the following sheets into the computer program

The forms that print out look like this:

# FBA DATA COLLECTION

**STUDENT:** Ralph Cunningham
**GR:** 10  **TCHR:** Joe Cool

| | Context (Setting) | | Antecedent Event | | Behavior | | Consequence | | Student Reaction |
|---|---|---|---|---|---|---|---|---|---|
| A | Home Room | A | Transition | A | Verbal Outburst | A | redirection | A | Stopped |
| B | English | B | Denied Access | B | Verbal Aggression | B | told no | B | Continued |
| C | Math | C | Instruction/Directive | C | Physical Aggression | C | sent to office | C | Intensified |
| D | Science | D | New Task | | | D | discussion of behavior | | |
| E | Physical Education | E | Tchr attn to other | | | E | choice given | | |
| F | Art | F | Told NO | | | F | peer attention | | |
| G | History | G | Choice given | | | G | Verbal reprimand | | |
| H | Reading | H | Waiting | | | H | ignored | | |
| I | Lunch Room | I | Quiet Work Time | | | | | | |
| J | Bus | J | Large Group Work | | | | | | |
| K | Hallway | K | Teacher Presenting | | | | | | |
| L | Office | L | New Material | | | | | | |

**Table of Contents**

Please note under the date - time of arrival if TARDY or time of departure if LEFT EARLY.

This page is READ ONLY. Changes must be done within the program. Return to Table of Contents.

| DATE | START TIME | END TIME | CONTEXT | ANTECEDENT | BEHAVIOR | CONSEQUENCE | STUDENT REACTION |
|---|---|---|---|---|---|---|---|
| | | | | | | | |
| | | | | | | | |
| | | | | | | | |
| | | | | | | | |
| | | | | | | | |
| | | | | | | | |
| | | | | | | | |
| | | | | | | | |
| | | | | | | | |
| | | | | | | | |
| | | | | | | | |
| | | | | | | | |
| | | | | | | | |
| | | | | | | | |
| | | | | | | | |
| | | | | | | | |
| | | | | | | | |

For data entering purposes- we will make it larger and easier to read in this context

August 20

| Time Begin | Time End | Context | Antecedent | Behavior | Consequence | Reaction |
|---|---|---|---|---|---|---|
| 8:15 | 8:17 | K | A | B | G | A |
| 12:50 | 12:51 | F | A | B | D | A |
| 12:55 | 1:07 | F | H | A | C | B |
| 1:55 | 1:57 | G | C | A | F | A |
| 2:03 | 2:07 | G | H | A | F | A |
| 2:47 | 2:49 | H | D | B | C | A |
| 2:54 | 2:55 | L | G | C | G | A |

ENTER THIS DATA- THEN GO BACK TO CALENDAR AND CLICK ON AUGUST 21- MAKE SURE YOU HAVE GREEN CHECKS BY EACH ROW AND THAT THERE IS A GREEN CHECK IN THE CALENDAR BOX. y

August 21

| Time Begin | Time End | Context | Antecedent | Behavior | Consequence | Reaction |
|---|---|---|---|---|---|---|
| 8:15 | 8:17 | K | A | B | G | A |
| 10:16 | 10:17 | K | A | A | D | A |
| 11:16 | 11:17 | C | D | C | C | A |

August 22

| Time Begin | Time End | Context | Antecedent | Behavior | Consequence | Reaction |
|---|---|---|---|---|---|---|
| 8:19 | 8:20 | K | A | B | G | A |
| 2:47 | 2:48 | H | D | C | C | A |
| 2:49 | 2:50 | K | A | B | A | A |

August 23

| Time Begin | Time End | Context | Antecedent | Behavior | Consequence | Reaction |
|---|---|---|---|---|---|---|
| 8:17 | 8:18 | K | A | B | G | A |
| 11:17 | 11:18 | K | A | B | D | A |
| 11:47 | 11:49 | I | E | A | F | A |
| 1:47 | 1:49 | K | A | B | G | A |
| 3:31 | 3:34 | G | H | C | C | A |

August 24

| Time Begin | Time End | Context | Antecedent | Behavior | Consequence | Reaction |
|---|---|---|---|---|---|---|
| 8:22 | 8:24 | K | A | B | G | A |
| 12:50 | 12:52 | F | A | B | D | A |
| 1:55 | 1:57 | H | D | B | C | A |
| 2:47 | 2:49 | G | C | A | F | A |

August 27

| Time Begin | Time End | Context | Antecedent | Behavior | Consequence | Reaction |
|---|---|---|---|---|---|---|
| 8:15 | 8:17 | K | A | B | G | A |
| 1:47 | 1:49 | G | H | C | C | A |
| 1:50 | 1:52 | G | C | A | F | A |
| 2:37 | 2:38 | K | A | B | G | A |

August 28

| Time Begin | Time End | Context | Antecedent | Behavior | Consequence | Reaction |
|---|---|---|---|---|---|---|
| 8:22 | 8:24 | K | A | B | D | A |
| 2:54 | 2:55 | L | G | C | C | A |
| 3:31 | 3:41 | K | A | A | F | A |

August 29

| Time Begin | Time End | Context | Antecedent | Behavior | Consequence | Reaction |
|---|---|---|---|---|---|---|
| 8:15 | 8:16 | K | A | B | G | A |
| 9:56 | 9:57 | C | D | C | C | A |
| 12:47 | 12:48 | K | A | B | D | A |
| 1:49 | 1:51 | G | D | C | C | A |
| 2:47 | 2:48 | H | H | A | F | A |

August 30

| Time Begin | Time End | Context | Antecedent | Behavior | Consequence | Reaction |
|---|---|---|---|---|---|---|
| 8:20 | 8:21 | K | A | B | G | A |
| 8:55 | 8:57 | B | D | C | C | A |
| 2:03 | 2:04 | G | H | A | F | A |

August 31

| Time Begin | Time End | Context | Antecedent | Behavior | Consequence | Reaction |
|---|---|---|---|---|---|---|
| 8:17 | 8:19 | K | A | B | G | A |
| 10:16 | 10:17 | C | D | C | C | A |
| 2:47 | 2:48 | H | D | C | C | A |
| 3:17 | 3:18 | H | H | A | F | A |

Now hit Report

Data Results from Ralph

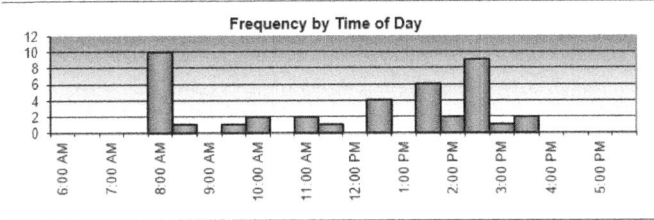

**Functional Behavior Assessment**

School: Monopoly School  Student: **Ralph Cunningham**
Grade: 10  School year: 2012 through 2013
Teacher: Joe Cool  Assessment period: Monday, August 20, 2012
Report prepared by: Snoop Dog

The purpose of this assessment is to determine the function of 3 target behaviors: verbal outburst; verbal aggression; physical aggression. Ralph was observed over a period of 10 school days. School was in session from 8:00 until 3:45.

**FREQUENCY OF BEHAVIORS** Each bar in the graph below represents the number of behaviors observed in each 30 minute time segment during this assessment period.

Most Active Times of Day

| | % of Total Activity | # of Events |
|---|---|---|
| 8:00 AM | 24% | 10 |
| 2:30 PM | 22% | 9 |

It's like watching a scary movie- "Don't go down in the basement!" You knew around 8:17 every morning the same sort of behavior was going to occur. ☺

8:00-8:30 and 2:30-3:00 are his two biggest target times of day.

Just from this information what would you do?

**BEHAVIORS PER DAY**

Ralph was assessed a total of 10 days.

Number of:
- Mondays: 2
- Tuesdays: 2
- Wednesdays: 2
- Thursdays: 2
- Fridays: 2

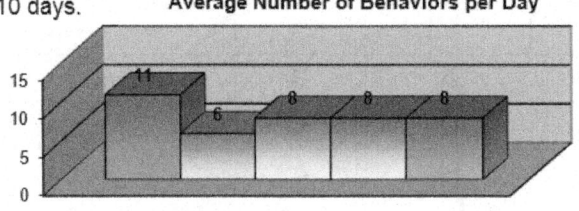

Average Number of Behaviors per Day

| Overall # of incidents | |
|---|---|
| Behavior A | 11 |
| Behavior B | 19 |
| Behavior C | 11 |
| Total | 41 |

Monday is his most difficult day of the week. How many of you have kids that have a really hard time on Monday? How many of you have a difficult time on Monday? Knowing this- what would you do in conjunction with the information in time of day?

This is his baseline information:

## The assessment period covered a total of 77:30 hours:min. Behaviors were charted 1:24 hr/min. This was 2% of the assessment period.

It's on your data sheet. He was observed for a total of 77.30 hours and he engaged in 1 hour and 24 minutes of behavior. This is 2% - We can measure this as baseline in several ways: Percent, Duration, or Frequency. We know the frequency from this data:

| Overall # of incidents | |
|---|---|
| Behavior A | 11 |
| Behavior B | 19 |
| Behavior C | 11 |
| Total | 41 |

We know the percent from this data:

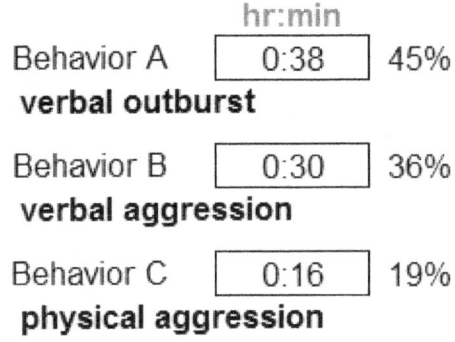

Behavior A  0:38  45%
**verbal outburst**

Behavior B  0:30  36%
**verbal aggression**

Behavior C  0:16  19%
**physical aggression**

**OVERALL:**  1:24
hr:min

We know duration from this data:

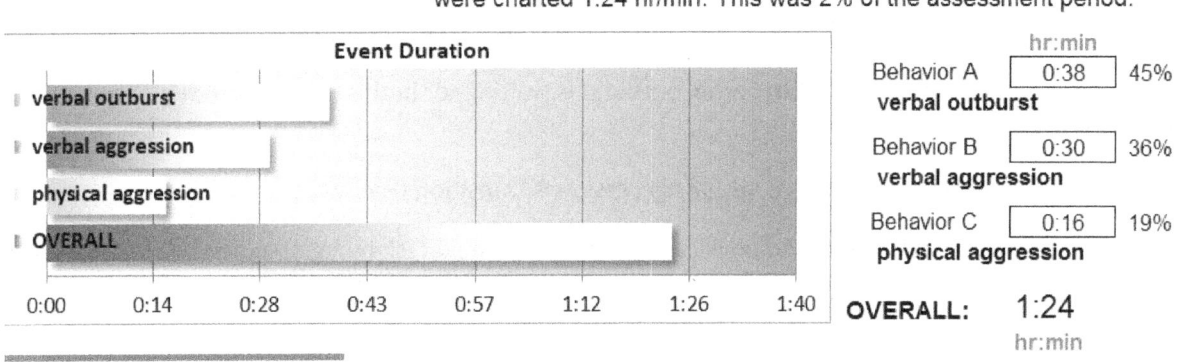

Now we want to look at the antecedent triggers (besides time of day and day of the week)

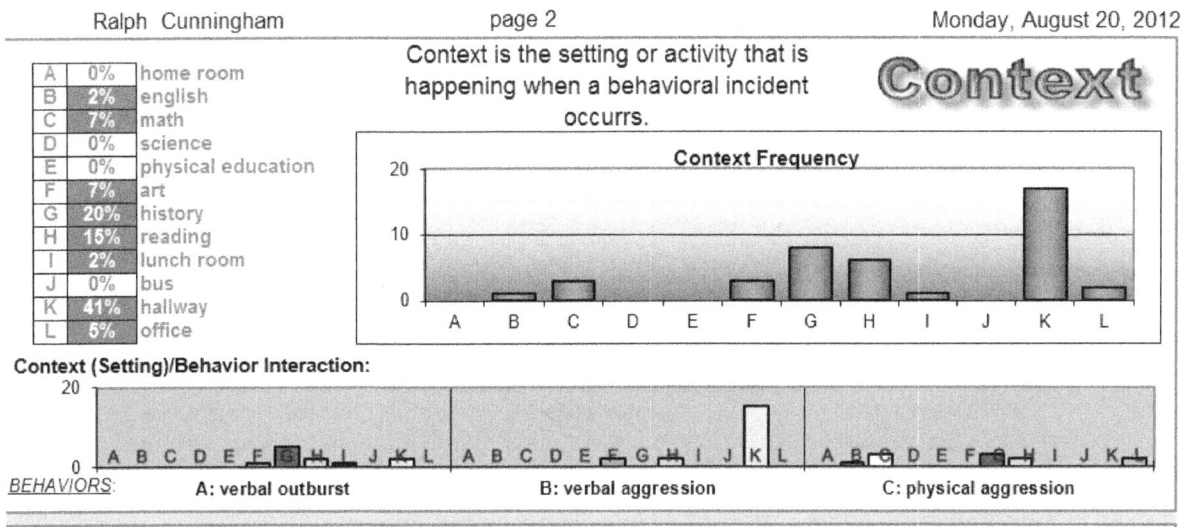

In context, we see that verbal outbursts most often are occurring in history class.

In context, we see that verbal aggression most often occurs in the hallway.

In context, we see that physical aggression most often occurs in history class as well.

So we have two areas: hallway and history class.

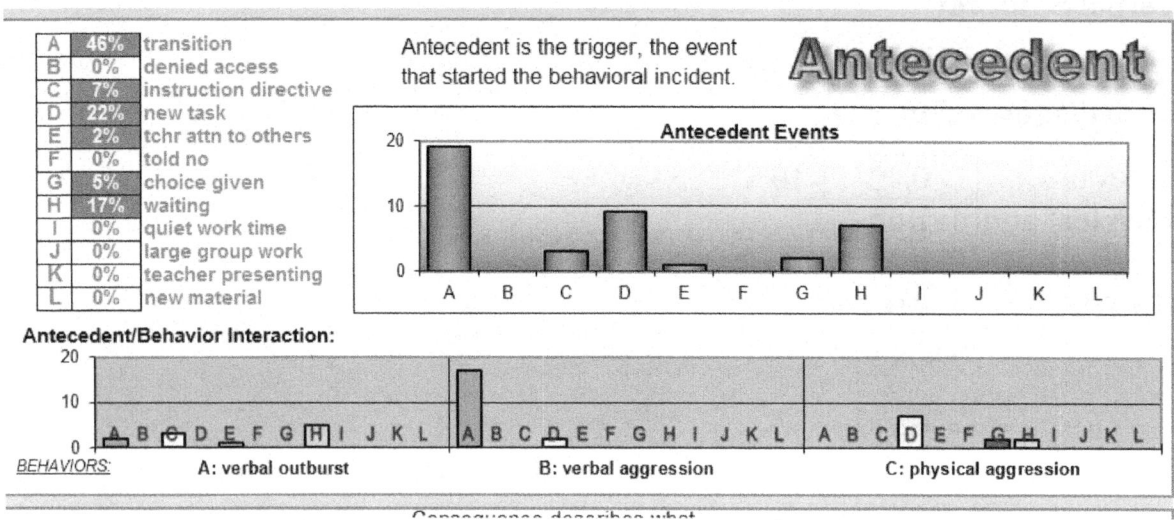

The antecedent most closely related to verbal outburst is waiting- or in this case "down time" (History Teacher is not well prepared).

The antecedent most closely related to verbal aggression is transition (Hallway).

The antecedent most closely related to physical aggression is a new task being assigned (History Class).

Now let's look at what is feeding these behaviors:

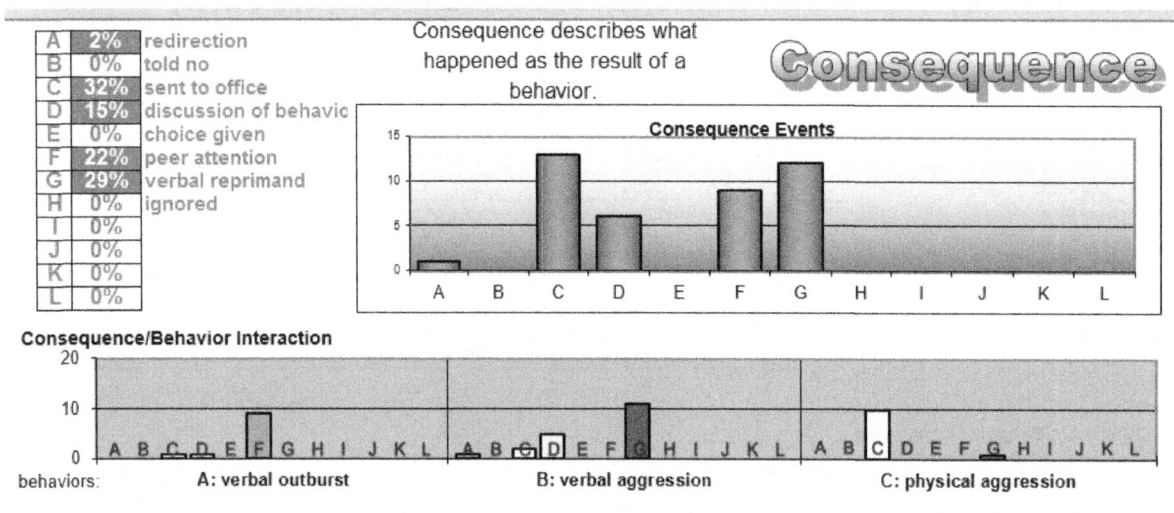

Verbal outburst seems to be fed by peer attention. So when there is down time in History class, Ralph tries to be a clown and use a verbal outburst to gain peer attention.

Verbal aggression seems to be fed by a verbal reprimand; this is adult attention and it most often occurs in the hallway during a transition. When Ralph is in the hall, he is verbally aggressive to certain students to gain adult attention. (He likes one adult in particular- based on anecdotal notes. Philip Quinn is the assistant principal and when Ralph sees him, he starts something with another student so Mr. Quinn will come over and talk to him.)

Physical aggression seems to be fed by being sent to the office which could be escape from a boring task or to gain attention from Mr. Philip Quinn who helps him with his work when he gets sent down. The team decided Ralph was getting both.

Now, we need to turn this into a competing pathway chart using our data. We need one chart for each function. For simplicity purposes- we are using a table formatted competing pathway chart on the next pages:

| Trigger | Target | impacT |
|---|---|---|
| Waiting/Down Time in History Class | Verbal Outburst | Peer Attention |
| **Revise the Environment** | **Replace the Behavior** | **Reframe the Response** |
| | | |
| Above- how would you set up the student for success knowing that waiting or down time triggers this behavior? | Above- What would you teach Ralph to do to replace the behaviors you are targeting? | Above- What would the adults do different to feed the replacement behavior and extinguish the target behavior? |

| Trigger | Target | impacT |
|---|---|---|
| Transition in the Hallway | Verbal Aggression | Adult Attention |
| **Revise the Environment** | **Replace the Behavior** | **Reframe the Response** |
| (Be sure to put in a modification for that 8:17 hallway) | | |
| Above- how would you set up the student for success knowing that transitions trigger this event? | Above- What would you teach Ralph to do to replace the behaviors you are targeting? | Above- What would the adults do different to feed the replacement behavior and extinguish the target behavior? |

| Trigger | Target | impacT |
|---|---|---|
| New Task | Physical Aggression | Gain Attention from Mr. Quinn who helps him with his task (escape class) |
| **Revise the Environment** | **Replace the Behavior** | **Reframe the Response** |
|  |  |  |
| Above- how would you set up the student for success knowing that new tasks trigger this event? | Above- What would you teach Ralph to do to replace the behaviors you are targeting? | Above- What would the adults do different to feed the replacement behavior and extinguish the target behavior? |

# Data Collection Tools:

# Behavior Count – Description, Procedures, & Example

When the behavior that you are looking at can be easily counted Behavior Count may be the best method to use, as it does not require too much effort and may not interfere with ongoing activities. A behavior can be easily counted when:
- The behavior has a clear beginning and end so that you can easily tell when the behavior starts and when it ends, <u>and</u>
- It does not happen at such a high rate that it is hard to keep track of.

There are several ways to keep track of behaviors as they occur: You can use a wrist counter; put paperclips, pennies, or buttons in one pocket and move them to a different "target" pocket as each behavior occurs; or make tally marks on a piece of paper. To obtain the total number of times that the behavior occurred, at the end of your observation time, you would either look at your wrist counter or add up the number of items in the "target" pocket, or the number of tally marks. This form uses tally marks. However, you can choose a different method to keep track of behaviors as they occur.

Examples of behaviors that you can measure by counting include leaving one's seat, raising one's hand, yelling out an answer, asking to go to the bathroom, being late or being on time to class, ….

## Procedures
<u>At the meeting</u>:

* Write down the behavior that you will be looking for and its definition
* If the team decides on an intervention (meetings 2 or 3), enter it in the box provided (p. 2)

<u>After the meeting</u>:

* Every time that you are "on the lookout" for the behavior:
  - Write down the date
  - Make a tally mark every time that the behavior occurs
  - At the end of your observation period, total the number of tally marks for that day (if using a different method to keep track of behavior, enter the total in the Total column) **(This is what you graph)**

## Example
<u>Behavior</u>: Leaving seat during class time

<u>Behavior Definition</u>: Being at least one foot away from desk/seat during class, any time after tardy bell rings. Includes times when has asked for permission to leave seat. See tally sheet on next page.

| Date | Tally every time that the behavior occurs | Total number of times behavior occurred |
|------|-------------------------------------------|------------------------------------------|
| 11/5 | ⊤⊦⊦⊥ \| \|                                | 7 |
| 11/6 | \| \| \| \|                               | 4 |
| 11/7 | ⊤⊦⊦⊥ \|                                   | 6 |
| 11/8 | ⊤⊦⊦⊥                                      | 5 |
| 11/9 | ⊤⊦⊦⊥ \| \| \|                             | 8 |

## Behavior Duration – Description, Procedures, & Example

If you are interested in measuring how long a behavior lasts you can do that by using the Behavior Duration method. However, in order to do so, you need to make sure that the behavior that you are looking at has a clear beginning and a clear ending so that you can tell exactly when the behavior starts and when it finishes. You will also need some timing instrument such as a wall clock, wristwatch, or stopwatch.

Examples of behaviors that you might want to measure the length of include crying, being out of the classroom, being in a particular location of the classroom, ....

**Procedures**

At the meeting:

* Write down the behavior that you will be looking for and its definition
* If the team decides on an intervention (meetings 2 or 3), enter it in the box provided (p. 2)

After the meeting:

* Make sure that you have your timing instrument available prior to beginning your observation
* Each time that the behavior occurs:
  - Write down the date
  - Write down the time when the behavior began
  - Write down the time when the behavior stopped
  - Calculate the length of time that the behavior lasted and write it in minutes and/or seconds **(This is what you graph)**

**Example**
Behavior: Working individually

Behavior Definition: Sitting at desk, with an assignment on the desk, looking at assignment, not talking to peers. Once student looks up (not looking at assignment any more), the behavior has stopped. If student begins talking to peers while looking at assignment, behavior has stopped.

| Date | Enter time when the behavior began | Enter time when behavior stopped | Length of time that the behavior lasted for |
|---|---|---|---|
| 11/5 | 9:55 AM | 10:06 AM | 11 minutes |
| 11/5 | 10:19 AM | 10:28 AM | 9 minutes |
| 11/6 | 9:43 AM | 9:51 AM | 8 minutes |
| 11/7 | 10:04 AM | 10:19 AM | 15 minutes |
| 11/7 | 10:23 AM | 10:33 AM | 10 minutes |

| 8:00 | 9:00 | 10:00 | 11:00 | 12:00 | 1:00 | 2:00 | 3:00 | 4:00 | 5:00 | 6:00 | 7:00 |
|---|---|---|---|---|---|---|---|---|---|---|---|
| 8:01 | 9:01 | 10:01 | 11:01 | 12:01 | 1:01 | 2:01 | 3:01 | 4:01 | 5:01 | 6:01 | 7:01 |
| 8:02 | 9:02 | 10:02 | 11:02 | 12:02 | 1:02 | 2:02 | 3:02 | 4:02 | 5:02 | 6:02 | 7:02 |
| 8:03 | 9:03 | 10:03 | 11:03 | 12:03 | 1:03 | 2:03 | 3:03 | 4:03 | 5:03 | 6:03 | 7:03 |
| 8:04 | 9:04 | 10:04 | 11:04 | 12:04 | 1:04 | 2:04 | 3:04 | 4:04 | 5:04 | 6:04 | 7:04 |
| 8:05 | 9:05 | 10:05 | 11:05 | 12:05 | 1:05 | 2:05 | 3:05 | 4:05 | 5:05 | 6:05 | 7:05 |
| 8:06 | 9:06 | 10:06 | 11:06 | 12:06 | 1:06 | 2:06 | 3:06 | 4:06 | 5:06 | 6:06 | 7:06 |
| 8:07 | 9:07 | 10:07 | 11:07 | 12:07 | 1:07 | 2:07 | 3:07 | 4:07 | 5:07 | 6:07 | 7:07 |
| 8:08 | 9:08 | 10:08 | 11:08 | 12:08 | 1:08 | 2:08 | 3:08 | 4:08 | 5:08 | 6:08 | 7:08 |
| 8:09 | 9:09 | 10:09 | 11:09 | 12:09 | 1:09 | 2:09 | 3:09 | 4:09 | 5:09 | 6:09 | 7:09 |
| 8:10 | 9:10 | 10:10 | 11:10 | 12:10 | 1:10 | 2:10 | 3:10 | 4:10 | 5:10 | 6:10 | 7:10 |
| 8:11 | 9:11 | 10:11 | 11:11 | 12:11 | 1:11 | 2:11 | 3:11 | 4:11 | 5:11 | 6:11 | 7:11 |
| 8:12 | 9:12 | 10:12 | 11:12 | 12:12 | 1:12 | 2:12 | 3:12 | 4:12 | 5:12 | 6:12 | 7:12 |
| 8:13 | 9:13 | 10:13 | 11:13 | 12:13 | 1:13 | 2:13 | 3:13 | 4:13 | 5:13 | 6:13 | 7:13 |
| 8:14 | 9:14 | 10:14 | 11:14 | 12:14 | 1:14 | 2:14 | 3:14 | 4:14 | 5:14 | 6:14 | 7:14 |
| 8:15 | 9:15 | 10:15 | 11:15 | 12:15 | 1:15 | 2:15 | 3:15 | 4:15 | 5:15 | 6:15 | 7:15 |
| 8:16 | 9:16 | 10:16 | 11:16 | 12:16 | 1:16 | 2:16 | 3:16 | 4:16 | 5:16 | 6:16 | 7:16 |
| 8:17 | 9:17 | 10:17 | 11:17 | 12:17 | 1:17 | 2:17 | 3:17 | 4:17 | 5:17 | 6:17 | 7:17 |
| 8:18 | 9:18 | 10:18 | 11:18 | 12:18 | 1:18 | 2:18 | 3:18 | 4:18 | 5:18 | 6:18 | 7:18 |
| 8:19 | 9:19 | 10:19 | 11:19 | 12:19 | 1:19 | 2:19 | 3:19 | 4:19 | 5:19 | 6:19 | 7:19 |
| 8:20 | 9:20 | 10:20 | 11:20 | 12:20 | 1:20 | 2:20 | 3:20 | 4:20 | 5:20 | 6:20 | 7:20 |
| 8:21 | 9:21 | 10:21 | 11:21 | 12:21 | 1:21 | 2:21 | 3:21 | 4:21 | 5:21 | 6:21 | 7:21 |
| 8:22 | 9:22 | 10:22 | 11:22 | 12:22 | 1:22 | 2:22 | 3:22 | 4:22 | 5:22 | 6:22 | 7:22 |
| 8:23 | 9:23 | 10:23 | 11:23 | 12:23 | 1:23 | 2:23 | 3:23 | 4:23 | 5:23 | 6:23 | 7:23 |
| 8:24 | 9:24 | 10:24 | 11:24 | 12:24 | 1:24 | 2:24 | 3:24 | 4:24 | 5:24 | 6:24 | 7:24 |
| 8:25 | 9:25 | 10:25 | 11:25 | 12:25 | 1:25 | 2:25 | 3:25 | 4:25 | 5:25 | 6:25 | 7:25 |
| 8:26 | 9:26 | 10:26 | 11:26 | 12:26 | 1:26 | 2:26 | 3:26 | 4:26 | 5:26 | 6:26 | 7:26 |
| 8:27 | 9:27 | 10:27 | 11:27 | 12:27 | 1:27 | 2:27 | 3:27 | 4:27 | 5:27 | 6:27 | 7:27 |
| 8:28 | 9:28 | 10:28 | 11:28 | 12:28 | 1:28 | 2:28 | 3:28 | 4:28 | 5:28 | 6:28 | 7:28 |
| 8:29 | 9:29 | 10:29 | 11:29 | 12:29 | 1:29 | 2:29 | 3:29 | 4:29 | 5:29 | 6:29 | 7:29 |
| 8:30 | 9:30 | 10:30 | 11:30 | 12:30 | 1:30 | 2:30 | 3:30 | 4:30 | 5:30 | 6:30 | 7:30 |
| 8:31 | 9:31 | 10:31 | 11:31 | 12:31 | 1:31 | 2:31 | 3:31 | 4:31 | 5:31 | 6:31 | 7:31 |
| 8:32 | 9:32 | 10:32 | 11:32 | 12:32 | 1:32 | 2:32 | 3:32 | 4:32 | 5:32 | 6:32 | 7:32 |
| 8:33 | 9:33 | 10:33 | 11:33 | 12:33 | 1:33 | 2:33 | 3:33 | 4:33 | 5:33 | 6:33 | 7:33 |
| 8:34 | 9:34 | 10:34 | 11:34 | 12:34 | 1:34 | 2:34 | 3:34 | 4:34 | 5:34 | 6:34 | 7:34 |
| 8:35 | 9:35 | 10:35 | 11:35 | 12:35 | 1:35 | 2:35 | 3:35 | 4:35 | 5:35 | 6:35 | 7:35 |
| 8:36 | 9:36 | 10:36 | 11:36 | 12:36 | 1:36 | 2:36 | 3:36 | 4:36 | 5:36 | 6:36 | 7:36 |
| 8:37 | 9:37 | 10:37 | 11:37 | 12:37 | 1:37 | 2:37 | 3:37 | 4:37 | 5:37 | 6:37 | 7:37 |
| 8:38 | 9:38 | 10:38 | 11:38 | 12:38 | 1:38 | 2:38 | 3:38 | 4:38 | 5:38 | 6:38 | 7:38 |
| 8:39 | 9:39 | 10:39 | 11:39 | 12:39 | 1:39 | 2:39 | 3:39 | 4:39 | 5:39 | 6:39 | 7:39 |
| 8:40 | 9:40 | 10:40 | 11:40 | 12:40 | 1:40 | 2:40 | 3:40 | 4:40 | 5:40 | 6:40 | 7:40 |
| 8:41 | 9:41 | 10:41 | 11:41 | 12:41 | 1:41 | 2:41 | 3:41 | 4:41 | 5:41 | 6:41 | 7:41 |
| 8:42 | 9:42 | 10:42 | 11:42 | 12:42 | 1:42 | 2:42 | 3:42 | 4:42 | 5:42 | 6:42 | 7:42 |
| 8:43 | 9:43 | 10:43 | 11:43 | 12:43 | 1:43 | 2:43 | 3:43 | 4:43 | 5:43 | 6:43 | 7:43 |
| 8:44 | 9:44 | 10:44 | 11:44 | 12:44 | 1:44 | 2:44 | 3:44 | 4:44 | 5:44 | 6:44 | 7:44 |
| 8:45 | 9:45 | 10:45 | 11:45 | 12:45 | 1:45 | 2:45 | 3:45 | 4:45 | 5:45 | 6:45 | 7:45 |
| 8:46 | 9:46 | 10:46 | 11:46 | 12:46 | 1:46 | 2:46 | 3:46 | 4:46 | 5:46 | 6:46 | 7:46 |
| 8:47 | 9:47 | 10:47 | 11:47 | 12:47 | 1:47 | 2:47 | 3:47 | 4:47 | 5:47 | 6:47 | 7:47 |
| 8:48 | 9:48 | 10:48 | 11:48 | 12:48 | 1:48 | 2:48 | 3:48 | 4:48 | 5:48 | 6:48 | 7:48 |
| 8:49 | 9:49 | 10:49 | 11:49 | 12:49 | 1:49 | 2:49 | 3:49 | 4:49 | 5:49 | 6:49 | 7:49 |
| 8:50 | 9:50 | 10:50 | 11:50 | 12:50 | 1:50 | 2:50 | 3:50 | 4:50 | 5:50 | 6:50 | 7:50 |
| 8:51 | 9:51 | 10:51 | 11:51 | 12:51 | 1:51 | 2:51 | 3:51 | 4:51 | 5:51 | 6:51 | 7:51 |
| 8:52 | 9:52 | 10:52 | 11:52 | 12:52 | 1:52 | 2:52 | 3:52 | 4:52 | 5:52 | 6:52 | 7:52 |
| 8:53 | 9:53 | 10:53 | 11:53 | 12:53 | 1:53 | 2:53 | 3:53 | 4:53 | 5:53 | 6:53 | 7:53 |
| 8:54 | 9:54 | 10:54 | 11:54 | 12:54 | 1:54 | 2:54 | 3:54 | 4:54 | 5:54 | 6:54 | 7:54 |
| 8:55 | 9:55 | 10:55 | 11:55 | 12:55 | 1:55 | 2:55 | 3:55 | 4:55 | 5:55 | 6:55 | 7:55 |
| 8:56 | 9:56 | 10:56 | 11:56 | 12:56 | 1:56 | 2:56 | 3:56 | 4:56 | 5:56 | 6:56 | 7:56 |
| 8:57 | 9:57 | 10:57 | 11:57 | 12:57 | 1:57 | 2:57 | 3:57 | 4:57 | 5:57 | 6:57 | 7:57 |
| 8:58 | 9:58 | 10:58 | 11:58 | 12:58 | 1:58 | 2:58 | 3:58 | 4:58 | 5:58 | 6:58 | 7:58 |
| 8:59 | 9:59 | 10:59 | 11:59 | 12:59 | 1:59 | 2:59 | 3:59 | 4:59 | 5:59 | 6:59 | 7:59 |

Minute by Minute Sheet    Date: _____    Student: _____

Behavior Doctor Seminars®™    2016-17 FY17 ©

# ON-TASK DATA SHEET

**STUDENT:**  PAGE: _____ OF _____

**DATE:**

**SAMPLING:** Partial interval system (15 seconds observation, followed by 5 seconds recording time).

**ACTIVITY:**  END TIME:

| START TIME | INTERVAL # | ON-TASK | OFF-TASK | NOT RATED |
|---|---|---|---|---|
| | 1 | | | |
| | 2 | | | |
| | 3 | | | |
| | 4 | | | |
| | 5 | | | |
| | 6 | | | |
| | 7 | | | |
| | 8 | | | |
| | 9 | | | |
| | 10 | | | |
| | 11 | | | |
| | 12 | | | |
| | 13 | | | |
| | 14 | | | |
| | 15 | | | |
| | 16 | | | |
| | 17 | | | |
| | 18 | | | |

## Daily Behavioral Frequency Sheet

**Student:**     **Target Behavior:**  Non-Compliance (see definition)

| Compliance | Total | Non-Compliance | Total | Time and Request/Activity |
|---|---|---|---|---|
| ☐☐☐☐☐☐☐ ☐☐☐☐☐☐☐ | | ☐☐☐☐☐☐☐ ☐☐☐☐☐☐☐ | | |
| ☐☐☐☐☐☐☐ ☐☐☐☐☐☐☐ | | ☐☐☐☐☐☐☐ ☐☐☐☐☐☐☐ | | |
| ☐☐☐☐☐☐☐ ☐☐☐☐☐☐☐ | | ☐☐☐☐☐☐☐ ☐☐☐☐☐☐☐ | | |
| ☐☐☐☐☐☐☐ ☐☐☐☐☐☐☐ | | ☐☐☐☐☐☐☐ ☐☐☐☐☐☐☐ | | |
| ☐☐☐☐☐☐☐ ☐☐☐☐☐☐☐ | | ☐☐☐☐☐☐☐ ☐☐☐☐☐☐☐ | | |
| Totals | | | | |

Behavior Doctor Seminars®™     2016-17 FY17 ©

# Partial Interval – Description, Procedures, & Example

When the behavior that you are looking at is not easily counted, you can measure the behavior by counting the number of time-intervals in which the behavior occurred. A behavior is not easily counted when:
- It is difficult to tell exactly when the behavior begins or when it ends, <u>or</u>
- It occurs at such a high rate that it is difficult to keep a count on it.

If this behavior happens so quickly that it is hard to catch (the behavior itself does not last for a long time), you may use the Partial Interval method to measure this behavior: You can look to see whether or not the behavior occurs at some point in each time interval. You should note that you will need some timing instrument such as a wall clock, wristwatch, or stopwatch in order to keep track of the time intervals.

Examples of behaviors that you can measure using Partial Interval include praising others, making a particular comment, making a certain gesture, walking by a particular place, ….

## Procedures

<u>At the meeting</u>:

* Write down the behavior that you will be looking for and its definition
* Write down how long you will be observing every time: Total Observation Time
* Divide the total observation time into 10 same length intervals; write down the length of each interval
    - All intervals need to be the same length: Intervals can be from a few seconds long up to a few minutes long (less than 11 minutes)
    
    **Note: Total observation time and length of intervals need to be the same each time that you observe**

* If the team decides on an intervention (meetings 2 or 3), enter it in the box provided (p. 2)

<u>After the meeting</u>:

* Enter the date of your observation
* Make sure that you have your timing instrument available prior to beginning your observation
* Keep an eye on your timing instrument to keep track of the intervals
* **During each time interval:**
    - Look to see if the behavior occurs
    - Once the behavior occurs, place a checkmark (✓) for that interval
    - If, at the end of the interval the behavior did not occur, place an X for that interval
* At the end of your observation time, total the number of checkmarks **(This is what you graph)**

## Example

<u>Behavior</u>: Saying something nice

<u>Behavior Definition</u>: Making a statement to a peer or a teacher during class time, in a pleasant tone, which includes either praise or politeness, for example saying "you did well" or "excuse me"

<u>Total Observation Time</u>: 20 minutes             <u>Length of each interval</u>: 2 minutes

| Date | Interval # | | | | | | | | | | Total times behavior occurred (✓) |
|---|---|---|---|---|---|---|---|---|---|---|---|
| 11/5 | 1 | 2 | 3 | 4 | 5 | 6 | 7 | 8 | 9 | 10 | |
| ✓ or X | ✓ | X | X | ✓ | X | X | X | ✓ | X | X | 3 |

Behavior Doctor Seminars®™    2016-17 FY17 ©

Student Name: _____ Date: _____

| ACTIVITY | PROMPTS (Includes verbal or physical) | BEHAVIORS **A**-Aggression **D**-Destructive acts **I**-Inappropriate language | T O T A L |
|---|---|---|---|
| BREAKFAST | ooooooooooooooooo | | |
| HOME ROOM | ooooooooooooooooo | | |
| MATH/CLAIBORNE | ooooooooooooooooo | | |
| SPECIALS (     ) | ooooooooooooooooo | | |
| MATH/CLAIBORNE | ooooooooooooooooo | | |
| LUNCH | ooooooooooooooooo | | |
| LANGUAGE ARTS | ooooooooooooooooo | | |
| SOCIAL STUDIES/SCIENCE | ooooooooooooooooo | | |
| LEISURE | ooooooooooooooooo | | |
| GYM (AFTER SCHOOL CARE) | ooooooooooooooooo | | |
| ACTIVITY: | ooooooooooooooooo | | |
| ACTIVITY: | ooooooooooooooooo | | |
| | | A-    D-    I- | |

Behavior Doctor Seminars®™   2016-17 FY17 ©

**Student Strengths:**

| Social | Academic |
|--------|----------|
|        |          |
|        |          |

**Student Needs:**

| Social | Academic |
|---|---|
|  |  |
|  |  |

FBA Data Tool

The FBA Data Tool will give you instantly graphed information to use with your behavior support team to make qualified hypotheses concerning the function behind the student's behavior.

## Functional Behavior Assessment

School: Morningstar Elementary
Grade: K   School year: 2011 through 2012
Teacher: Mrs. Eggle
Report prepared by: Mrs. Eggle

Student: **Maddie Jones**
Assessment period: Monday, August 8, 2011

The purpose of this assessment is to determine the function of 3 target behaviors: Tantrum; Off Task; Cussing. Maddie was observed over a period of 10 school days. School was in session from 8:00 until 3:30.

### FREQUENCY OF

Each bar in the graph below represents the number of behaviors observed in each 30 minute time segment during this assessment period.

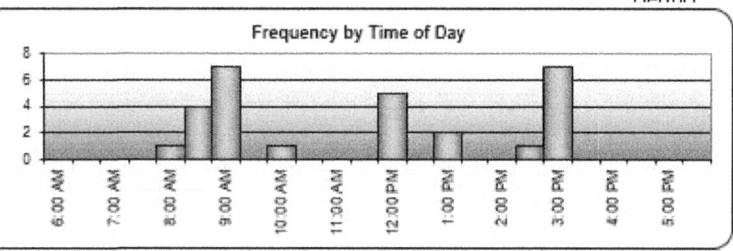

**Most Active Times of Day**

| | % of Total Activity | # of Events |
|---|---|---|
| 9:00 AM | 20% | 7 |
| 3:00 PM | 20% | 7 |
| 12:00 PM | 14% | 5 |

Total # of behavioral incidents: 19

### BEHAVIORS PER DAY

Maddie was assessed a total of 10 days.

Number of:  Mondays 2
            Tuesdays 2
            Wednesdays 2
            Thursdays 2
            Fridays 2

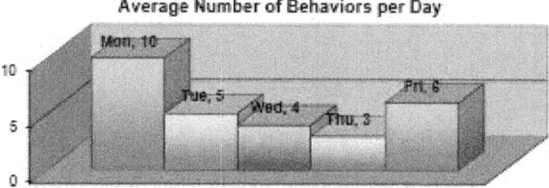

Average Number of Behaviors per Day
Mon, 10; Tue, 5; Wed, 4; Thu, 3; Fri, 6

We look to see if there are any triggers in time of day or day of the week. If there are- we fill them in on our worksheet.

| Trigger | Target | impacT |
|---|---|---|
| (jot down any triggers you see in time of day or day of the week.) | | |

54

Behavior Doctor Seminars®™   2016-17 FY17 ©

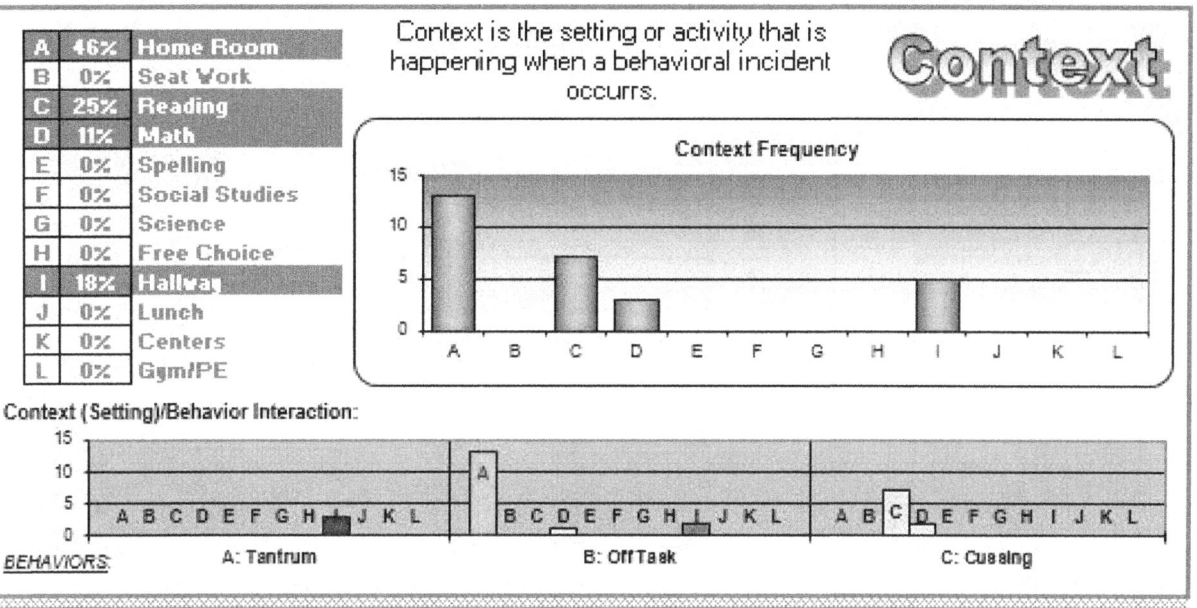

| Trigger | Target | impacT |
|---|---|---|
| (jot down any triggers you see in context/setting events.) | Be sure to note which behaviors have which triggers. | |

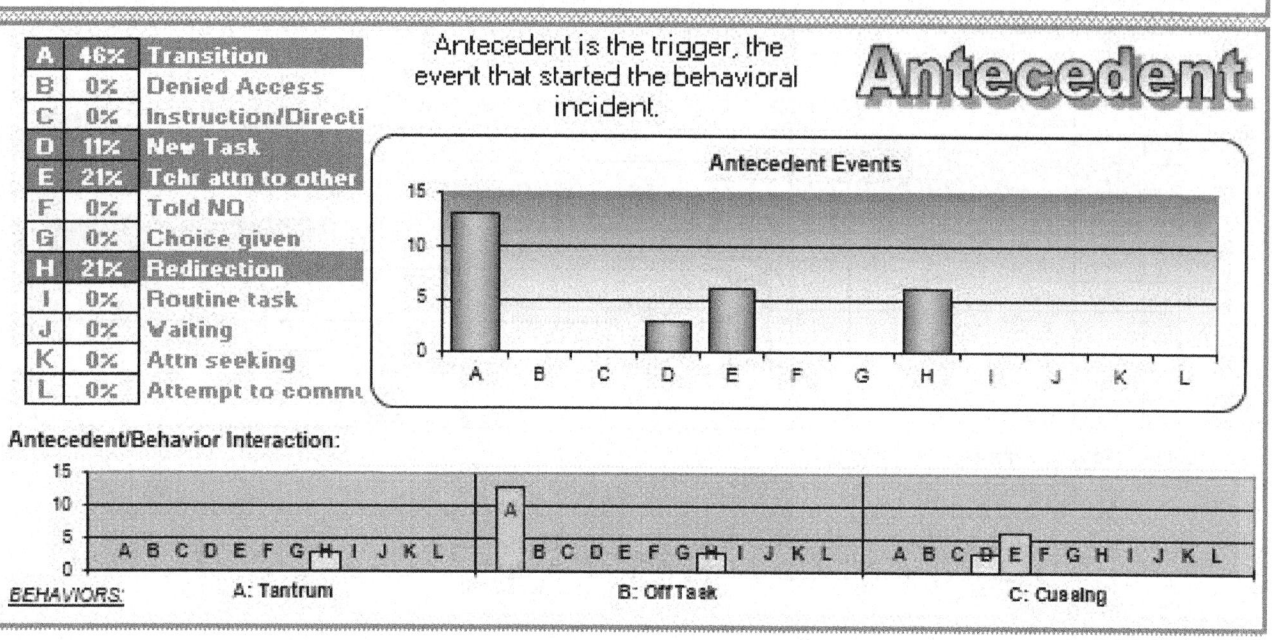

| Trigger | Target | impacT |
|---|---|---|
| (jot down any triggers you see in antecedent) | Be sure to note which behaviors seem to be paired with which triggers. | |

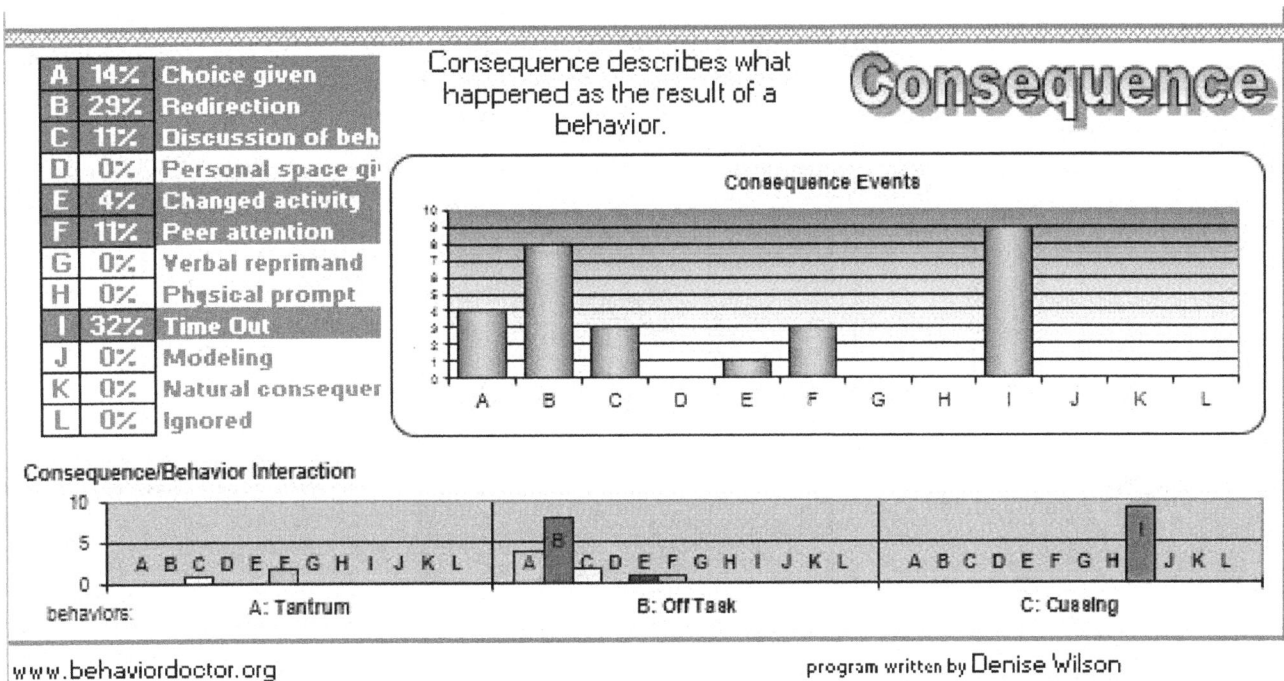

| Trigger | Target | impacT |
|---|---|---|
|  | Be sure to note which behaviors are fed by which consequences. | Now jot down any consequences that seem to be feeding the behaviors. |

Put it all together now and you have your summary statements:

The team can develop a summary statement from this information:

1) When Maddie is in the hallway, she is likely to have a tantrum to gain peer attention
2) When Maddie is having a transition, she is likely to be off task to gain adult attention
3) When Maddie has a new task or perceives she needs help and is not getting it, she is likely to cuss to gain escape from the task

**Triple T-Triple R Chart for Behavioral Intervention Planning:**

**Student Name:** _____ **Date:** _____

| Trigger | Target | impacT |
|---|---|---|
|  |  |  |
| **Revise the Environment** | **Replace the Behavior** | **Reframe the Response** |
|  |  |  |

**Triple T-Triple R Chart for Behavioral Intervention Planning:**

**Student Name:** _____ **Date:** _____

| Trigger | Target | impacT |
|---------|--------|--------|
|         |        |        |

| Revise the Environment | Replace the Behavior | Reframe the Response |
|------------------------|----------------------|----------------------|
|                        |                      |                      |

**Triple T-Triple R Chart for Behavioral Intervention Planning:**

**Student Name:** _____ **Date:** _____

| Trigger | Target | impacT |
|---|---|---|
|  |  |  |
| **Revise the Environment** | **Replace the Behavior** | **Reframe the Response** |
|  |  |  |

POSITIVE BEHAVIOR SUPPORT AT THE TERTIARY LEVEL

# Putting it All Together

Now that we have talked about all three strands of the braid, let's put in some of your students:

NAME: _____ DATE: _____

| Trigger | Target | impacT | Who is Responsible? (each item(s) may have different people responsible) |
|---|---|---|---|
|  |  |  |  |
| **Revision of the Environment** | **Replacing the Behavior** | **Reframing the Response** |  |
|  |  |  |  |

**Crisis Plan**: _____

Next Meeting Date: _____.

# Putting it All Together

NAME: _____ DATE: _____

| Trigger | Target | impacT | Who is Responsible? (each item(s) may have different people responsible) |
|---|---|---|---|
|  |  |  |  |
| **Revision of the Environment** | **Replacing the Behavior** | **Reframing the Response** |  |
|  |  |  |  |

**Crisis Plan:** _____

Next Meeting Date: _____.

# Putting it All Together

NAME: _____  DATE: _____

| Trigger | Target | impacT | Who is Responsible? (each item(s) may have different people responsible) |
|---------|--------|--------|---|
|         |        |        |   |
| **Revision of the Environment** | **Replacing the Behavior** | **Reframing the Response** | |
|         |        |        |   |

**Crisis Plan**: _____

Next Meeting Date: _____.

# Academic Struggles

— **Family Game Night**
http://tinyurl.com/planagamenight

> For students who are **struggling academically**. I taught in a school with over 400 students and typically when we had a parent night about 40-50 parents would show up and it was always the same 40-50 parents. We wrote a small grant and ordered tag board, markers, stickers, laminating film, dice, game markers etc. We made some templates for game boards and set up make-it/take-it centers for the families to come and make a game board. Each family would work together to color and decorate their game board. After getting their decorated game board laminated, each family was given game cards in accordance with the grade levels in their home. This way if they played the game as a family, the second grade student would hear advanced questions for the fourth grader and the fourth grader would hear review questions from the second grader. We had over 400 parents show up for this activity.

— **Mnemonics**
http://tinyurl.com/mnemonicspelling

http://tinyurl.com/meichenbaum

> **Academic Intervention for Spelling-**We all use mnemonics to help us: "Thirty days hath September…." "every good boy does fine". I used to give a pretest on Friday and I would take the top 5 missed spelling words and make up a mnemonic for each of those 5 words. I would teach that to the students the next week using Meichenbaum's 5 step cognitive learning theory.

— **Note Taking Technique/Helps Alleviate Wandering Minds**
http://tinyurl.com/notemakingtemplates

> **Academic Intervention** Dr. Andrew Fuller states notes should be divided into a chart with two rows. The top row is split in two- one side for the main idea and the other side for notes. The row underneath should be devoted to drawing pictures to help the students remember what was taught.

— **Parent Training**
http://www.pbis.org/training/parents.aspx

> **To help with academics and behavior**. Great ideas to get parents engaged- teach them how you want them to be involved. Ask them to donate one hour a month coming up to school and passing out gotchas to students they catch exhibiting appropriate behaviors, tutor students on math facts, listen to students read, etc.

— **Peer Tutoring**
http://www.nea.org/tools/35542.htm

> **To Increase Academics.** When instituting the Four P's for raising self-esteem, peer tutoring or philanthropy through helping others helps both students. Use your students

who struggle in their own grade to go down and tutor younger students or students with special needs. Surprisingly, they will feel better about themselves and not only help the students they are helping- they will help themselves.

- **PIRATES**

http://www.slideshare.net/monroeslc/pirates-test-taking-strategies

>**To help with academics**. I use PIRATES to introduce people to the Kansas Learning Strategies. http://www.ku-crl.org/sim/strategies.shtml - It's actually now called SIM – Strategic Intervention Model. Wonderful program.

- **Pre-Teaching Anticipatory Set**

http://tinyurl.com/anticipatorysets

>For students who struggle **academically**, as part of check-in/check-out, the student should be taught the answer to the anticipatory set question or activity. This will make the student feel like they know the answer to the next question.

- **Restructuring the Day**

http://tinyurl.com/dufourwit

>**Academic Intervention**. Weatherford High School restructured their day and built an extra 30 minutes into the day. Students get an hour for lunch. 30 minutes to eat and 30 minutes to do one of two things. If the student is making an A, B, or C they are allowed to take a fun class, study, work on computer projects. If the students are making a D or F they get to go spend a whole week with the teacher whose class, they are failing. Teachers love it because they get to work one on one or two with the students who are struggling and get them caught up.

- **Three Stars and a Wish**

http://tinyurl.com/3staronewish

>**Academic Improvement in Writing**. John Morris from Haversham England invented this. It can be used in two ways. One is with writing. Each piece that is turned in should have 3 stars (3 great things pointed out) and one wish- one thing to build on to redo the paper. The student keeps redoing the paper until it is perfect. Using same method each time.

--Social connection between students & adults

>The other way is to have the students write down three things that went well this week and one thing they wish had gone better. This is turned in to the teacher to learn what might be bothering the student and be able to intervene.

# Aggression

— **Hokey Pokey Clinic**
http://tinyurl.com/leftfootin

For **verbal and physical aggression**. This cannot be taught when the student is drunk on emotion. Teachers have to teach it and model it when the student is in control of their body. The Hokey Pokey Clinic is a place to go to turn yourself around. This is an area with a purple bulletin board with nature pictures and a blue wall (if you follow Feng Shui). The blue bean bag is in this area. Sixty beats per minute (BPM) music is playing on headphones or very softly for the entire room. The student will be given a Kleenex box (empty) with 20 fuzzy pompons. The student is taught to breathe-in-2-3-4 and breathe-out-2-3-4. (Tongue behind two front teeth and mouth closed). Breathing in and out through the nose. The student is to repeat this 10 in and 10 out by dropping a pompon in the box for each part of the cycle. This brings oxygen to the frontal cortex instead of the brain stem. Students are praised and given a token when they use this instead of getting upset. I like for the teacher to model it as well. Pretend he/she is upset about something like the computer not working correctly and go over and sit in the bean bag and breathe – counting each cycle of breathing by dropping the pompons into the Kleenex box.

— **Ice Cube Break**

For students who **lose their temper**. I give each of them one plastic ice cube with the word "break" written on it with a permanent marker. They are allowed to use it once per day. This is a hallway pass and the student is allowed to walk up and down the hallway 3 trips to calm themselves down before returning to class.

— **Power Cards**
http://tinyurl.com/powercards4bx

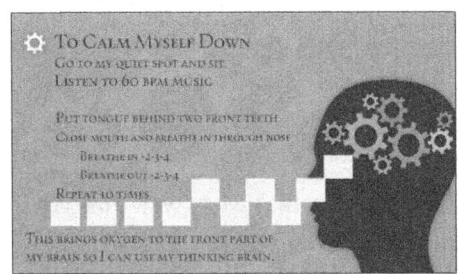 

**Verbal Aggression** is one of the behaviors you can address with a power card. The front of the card has a topic of interest to them- the back of the card tells them what to do when they are **angry, frustrated, or want attention.** I make 12 of them the first time and laminate them because the student will lose them from time to time- that way you have a spare.

 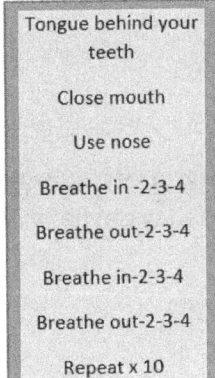

Front of card       back of card

You could also write: I feel _____ when _____. I need _____. As a sentence to help the student make their point in a more socially acceptable way.

## — Social Autopsy

http://www.ricklavoie.com/competart.html

**For aggression (mild), disruptive behaviors, or poor judgment in social skills.** Under materials download on www.behaviordoctor.org, I have samples of social autopsies. I like them so much better than think sheets because they focus on proactive changes for the student to think about paired with cues to use the sheet when needed.

# Anxiety

## — Acupressure
http://tinyurl.com/accupressure4kids

For **anxiety, stress, worrying**- When students feel their heart begin to race- here is a technique they can be taught to help themselves self-regulate:

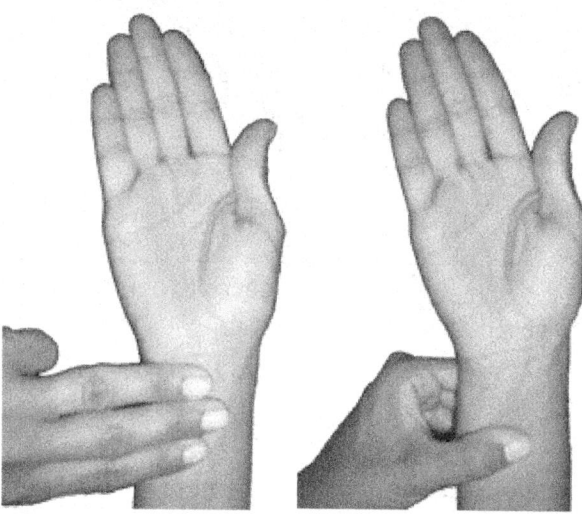

1. Measure    2. Apply Pressure

This slows down the heart rate and allows the student to calm down and focus on what is important. Whether or not you believe in acupressure, it works as a diversion which takes the student's mind off their anxious focus.

## — Blue Beanbag Calming Area
http://tinyurl.com/targetbeanbagblue

(request through www.donorschoose.org )

For **tantrums, anxiety, stress, verbal or physical aggression**. You might wonder why blue? In the philosophy of Feng Shui, blue is a calming color. I prefer a pleather beanbag for two reasons: 1) critter resistance and 2) it is cool to the touch. Students with anger issues, anxiety, stress, or aggression tend to have increased heart rates which increases their core body temperature. The bean bag is like a cool hug. At the point of being upset, a child cannot be hugged into good behavior. However, training them when they aren't upset to go to the blue beanbag and do their breathing exercises will help them calm themselves down.

## — Brain Gym
http://www.braingym.org/

https://www.alertprogram.com/

For **disorganization, anxiety, stress, sleepiness, and impulsiveness**. Brain Gym and the Alert program are two programs that teach students how to rev up their engines or slow their engines down. The program also has activities for connecting the right side of the brain with the left side of the brain and to get the synapses flowing before a test. They are great programs to use in the classroom.

## Check-in/Check-out
http://tinyurl.com/hawkencico

Check-in/Check-out is a wonderful program that can be used for **anxiety, self-esteem, disorganization, verbal outbursts, verbal aggression, physical aggression (before it begins), and lack of ownership.**

I really like the video produced by Dr. Leanne Hawken – the link is on the left. It's a great one to show the entire staff and discuss which students would benefit from using the system. It's geared for tier two students- however, it would be useful for those at risk students as well.

## Chewing Gum
http://tinyurl.com/chewgum4focus

For **anxiety, impulsivity, hyperacusis, and stress**.

- Chewing gum reduces anxiety
    - More socially acceptable than chewing on pencils, shirts etc.
    - Oral activity is calming
- Actually dulls background noise by activating the Eustachian tube for students who find it hard to focus in noisy classrooms.
    - Kids who chew gum during tests do 26% to 36% better.

## Dark Chocolate
http://tinyurl.com/darkchocolateisgood

For students with **anxiety, attention deficit hyperactive disorder (inattentive), and sleepiness**.

- Research indicates a small piece of dark chocolate boosts memory, alertness, and concentration, and its special chemicals even decrease anxiety.
- They sell small bite size bars of dark chocolate- especially on test days- pass them out.

## Good Breakfast (Eggs and Oatmeal)
http://tinyurl.com/eggsbrainfood

http://tinyurl.com/oatmealbrainfood

**To increase test scores**. Right before the high stakes tests- send home this information to parents. Breakfast is so important and what the students eat is even more important.

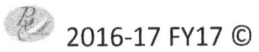

Don't skip breakfast. Students who eat breakfast score higher on tests and report less test-related anxiety. Best bets? Eggs for brain-boosting choline, and oatmeal for a calming increase in serotonin levels.

### ---Music (60bpm)
http://www.shortlist.com/entertainment/music/scientists-discover-most-relaxing-tune-ever

www.behaviordoctor.org- go to material download and check out videos.

**To decrease aggressive behaviors and alleviate anxiety:**

Music research tells us that our heart rates will match the music we are listening to. Also, research on students with aggressive behaviors tells us their heart rates jump up to 147 beats per minute (on average) a full 45-90 seconds prior to aggressive act. If we can intervene, by playing 60 bpm music (the resting heart rate), the students will be calmer.

### — Nature Pictures
http://behaviordoctor.org/calmingvideos.html

http://alexandria.tue.nl/extra2/afstversl/tm/De_Jonge_2011.pdf

**For students with anxiety.**

A University of Michigan research study found that looking at 7 minutes of nature pictures reduced anxiety before a test. The music link above is paired with nature pictures. You can show this before test with or without the music.

### — Refrigerator Tubing for Kids Who Chew on Pencils
http://www.nationalautismresources.com/cheweze.html

**Students who chew on their pencils because of anxiety.** Take a pencil with you to a lumber yard and ask where the refrigerator tubing is located. Figure out which one fits on the end of a pencil and purchase a yard or two of it. It's going to cost you less than $5. Push it on top of the pencil and cut it off even with the eraser. Then push it down a bit further so the eraser is free to be used. This will keep the student from chewing up the metal and chewing on the wood of the pencil. The tubing is food grade so it's safe.

### — Self-Calming Techniques
http://tinyurl.com/selfregulationtips

**Anxiety, Anger, or Stress.** Teach students how to calm themselves down using breathing techniques, stress balls, cognitive behavior modification etc.

### — Taking Off Shoes and Wiggling Toes
http://tinyurl.com/wiggleyourtoes

http://www.helpguide.org/mental/quick_stress_relief.htm

Taking off your shoes and wiggling your toes reduces **anxiety**. In Iceland, Korea, New Zealand, and Australia- I found the students were barefoot. Interesting that all these countries beat us in resilience and many times beat us in academic achievement.

— **Using Lavender to Decrease Anxiety**
http://www.naturalmedicinejournal.com/article_content.asp?article=289

**Decreasing Anxiety**. This is the research behind spritzing the room with lavender discussed earlier.

— **Walk and Talk**
http://www.calmclinic.com/anxiety/treatment/walking-works

**To Decrease Tantrums**. One of the best ways to calm a student down and give them some proprioceptive input is to allow them to walk around the hallways for a few minutes with an available adult. Just walk and talk-

— **Writing About Anxiety for Ten Minutes**
http://news.uchicago.edu/article/2011/01/13/writing-about-worries-eases-anxiety-and-improves-test-performance

**Anxiety**. The University of Chicago has found that writing about your anxiety for ten minutes reduces anxiety. Many teachers have the students do this and then take the writing and wad it up and throw it away- like "I'm done with worrying about that."

— **Yoga Breathing**
http://kidsyogaguide.com/

**Anxiety, Anger, Stress**. Teach students how to regulate themselves by using yoga breathing. It brings oxygen to the frontal cortex instead of leaving the student with only a brain stem to do the thinking.

# Apathy

— Banking Reinforcement System
http://www.handsonbanking.org/en/resources/Kids_T_Guide.pdf

For students with **apathy** toward schoolwork.

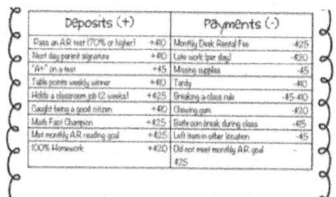

*photo from Pinterest

I combined behavior, social studies, & math. The students were paid for: Good behavior, Good grades, Returning items, Supplies etc.

The students were paid in the monetary system of the country we were studying and had to convert to US Dollars using current rates.

Each student had a checkbook- could purchase Reinforcements for self or whole class.

— **Games and Why They Are Your Friend**
http://tinyurl.com/realityisbrokengames

For students who do not seem to **pay attention, join in participation, or work independently**. Playing games in the classroom is an excellent way to "hook" them on learning. There are literally hundreds of beautiful game templates. If you type in a google search "games + PowerPoint template" the links will pop up. All you have to do is put in the question and answers and you can soon be playing "Are You Smarter Than a Fifth Grader?", "Who Wants to Be a Millionaire?", "Jeopardy" and many more. The students will be begging to play more and what they won't know is they are learning. Read some of the research on why games are so addictive in the book to the left.

- When we are playing a good game- when we're tackling unnecessary obstacles- we are actively moving ourselves toward the positive end of the emotional spectrum.
- Compared with games, reality is too easy. Games challenge us with voluntary obstacles and help us put our personal strengths to better use.
- Failure is fun. Games eliminate our fear of failure and improve our chances for success.
- Being really good at something is less fun than being not quite good enough-yet.
- Ten minutes of non-violent games quickens your thought processes. This lets you make decisions and see connections faster.
- Bonus:

- These games distract you from anxieties; which hampers quick thinking.

— **Lucky Seven (Price is Right)**
http://priceisright.wikia.com/wiki/Lucky_Seven

> To get **buy-in** from the students. This is a group vs. group contingency sample. Each team is given $7. (It's a price is right game). You ask review questions. Every time they get one wrong, they lose a dollar. They answer together as a team so it's not response cost or a punishment. They have to have $1 left to buy 5 answers to that day's assignment. The team that has $1 left gets to have 5 less problems than the other half of the class. Just a friendly competition.

— **Student Engagement**
http://tinyurl.com/studentengagementmaiers

> **Disengaged students**. It's so important to get kids hooked in. In the DuFour book on "Whatever it Takes", the authors talk about how important it is to make sure all the students are connected. Make sure you have enough clubs and organizations for all the students to join. One of the schools in the book requires all students to join a club.

— **Student Self-Progress Monitoring**
https://www.interventioncentral.org/self_management_self_monitoring

> **Low Academic or Behavioral Proficiency**. John Hattie says the number one intervention for changing behavior and academics is students monitoring their own progress.

— **Student Voice**
http://tinyurl.com/studentvoiceriffel

> **To increase student buy-in**. This was one of the most fun projects I ever engaged in for SWPBIS. We met with students and trained them before we trained the adults. We had the students attend the two-day training on PBIS. At first the principals were not happy about that idea- they ended up loving it and found out such great information from the students.

# Argumentative

- **Perhaps You Could Be Right**

    For students who like to **argue**- Come up with a set phrase that basically tells the student they could be right- but not taking the bait.

    Student: "You're a mean teacher."

    Teacher: "Perhaps, you could be right." Teacher goes right back to teaching.

# Bullying

### — Delete Bracelets
http://www.behaviordoctor.org/bullying.html

> To remind students not to **bully**. These bracelets are similar to the Lance Armstrong bracelets. Weatherford High School invented them. They give them to the students so they see it on their wrist when they are typing. It reminds to students to not post anything that isn't true, helpful, inspiring, necessary or kind.

### — Step-Up Program
http://ethics4schools.com/counseling/

> **Anti-bullying** program. I love this program. You will make a video using your own students. Check out this great bully proofing program. There is a song and a great presentation on what bullying really is.

### — Stop, Walk, and Talk
http://pbis.org/school/bully_prevention.aspx

http://tinyurl.com/stopwalktalk

> **Anti-bullying**. This is a free 49-page booklet you can download and use in your school to stop bullying within a PBIS school. It would work for any school- not just PBIS schools.

# Response Feedback

**— Saturday Detention- Not Out of School Suspension**
http://tinyurl.com/kykotc2

**Don't take away academics- take away extra-curricular activities.**
**Instead of out of school detentions**. I would like to see out of school detention outlawed. Most of the kids who get out of school detention- don't want to be at school anyway. (Well that's not exactly true- with all the zero tolerance over reactions that are going on- innocent children are being sent home). Case in point – a three-year-old suspended for 3 days for sneaking a cheese sandwich to school. A six-year-old being suspended for chewing his pop tart into the shape of a gun and saying "pew pew" now has a weapons charge on his record.

Assign Saturday detention- especially for kids who play sports on Saturday this will be a real deterrent.

# Disorganization

— **Address Labels**
http://tinyurl.com/templatelabelsavery

For **disorganization, students who cannot copy from a vertical plane to a horizontal plane, or students with whom you are differentiating homework assignments**. Print out all homework assignments on address labels and just give to students to put in agenda book- this alleviates the problem of students not writing it down and makes it imperceptible to others that one student's assignment is different.

> 3/15 Homework
> Interview your parents on how they use Math in their job- bring back four sentences or more.

— **Cell Phones- How to Use Them**
http://tinyurl.com/cellphoneastool

For **disorganization, apathy, not paying attention, lack of buy-in**.

Why fight it? We have students who buy a cheap phone to turn in at the front door and keep the good one in their backpack. These students can text with their hands in their pockets. Have students take pictures of diagrams on the board and email them to themselves to review before a test. Have students take pictures of the homework assignment and email it to themselves. Send them on scavenger hunts to find right angles, a topic for writing, a picture to write a story problem about etc. Use www.polleverywhere.com – the students will be asked questions and they will text their answer to the number you give them. A graph will appear on the board showing how many students chose answer A, B, C, or D. You can build this right into your powerpoints when reviewing for a test. The link on the left has a bunch of ideas for you.

--**Classroom Locker (Keep Supplies in Room/Home)**

For **disorganized** students. Sometimes, we have students who can't remember to take their books home for homework or bring them back when they do take them home. Rather than waste any class time or letting that student lose class time- I sent one book home to stay until the end of the year and kept the other in the classroom (secondary). I know people will say this isn't teaching them organizational skills. The truth is- how is what you are currently doing working out to keep the student in class? Being in my class learning is the most important goal- you don't get out of my class that easy.

— **Crates by the back door**
http://tinyurl.com/targetcrates

For students with **disorganization**. This is something to share with parents. Show parents how they can put a crate or basket by the back door. Ask the parents to have their children load the crate or basket the night before right before they go to bed. This way, the student is not running around in the morning trying to find their library book, tennis shoes for PE etc.

Picture property of aimee-weaver.blogspot.com- from Pinterest.

— **Desk Fairy/Locker Fairy**
http://tinyurl.com/lockerfairynotes

For **disorganized** students. Have the students draw a map of what their desk or locker is supposed to look like. Do spot checks and put a certificate in their desk or locker when you catch it looking good. I call it the desk fairy or the locker fairy and the fairy leaves the students a school supply prize. (special pencils, mechanical pencils, spiral notebooks, or erasers).

— **Luggage Tag**

For students with **disorganization**. I like to take a luggage tag from the dollar store and flip the address label over and write down all the things that should go inside the backpack- like a "to do" list. Give the student a dry erase marker to mark off items as they put them in. Also, if you have "A" day and "B" day etc. you can have different color cards and cue the students by telling them to flip their cards forward in the luggage tag. No more forgotten library books etc.

# Disruptive Outbursts

## — Behavior Specific Praise
http://www.mayinstitute.org/news/topic_center.html?id=932

### For **disruptive outbursts (non-aggressive)**

Good Job means nothing. You have to label appropriate behavior when you see it. I spy someone sitting up straight and tall and really paying attention. The more you do this- the more of that you will see. When you say, "Cut that out"- you are giving energy to the inappropriate behavior and therefore you see more of it. Give your energy to the positive behavior. Energy flows where attention goes.

## — Diversionary Tactics
http://tinyurl.com/divertbehavior

For **disruptive students (blurts, off task, non-compliant)**. Help teachers see that using a diversionary tactic is better than calling a student down for inappropriate behavior. Using the student's name in a math story problem, asking the student to do a task within the classroom, asking for every pupil response (EPR) will keep the student from remaining off task.

## --Ear Wiggle
http://www.ask.com/question/why-did-carol-burnett-tug-her-ear

http://tinyurl.com/curtaindress

### (secret signal to help a student save face)
For students with **disruptive** behaviors. Remember Carol Burnett? Some of you are too young. ☺ Every night at the end of her variety show, she would tug on her ear. It was a secret signal between her and her grandma to let her grandma know she was alright. I used this technique to signal to students what they needed to be doing. If I pulled on my ear, it meant- whatever I say next is what I need you to be doing. I would pull on my ear and then say- "I spy someone sitting up straight and tall and really paying attention." This way the student saved face by not being told to straighten up in front of their peers. The students typically straightened up after that.

## — Group vs. Group Contingency/Group Reinforcement
http://165.139.150.129/intervention/Group.pdf

To decrease **disruptions, non-compliance, and inattentiveness** pit the students against each other in a group vs group contingency reinforcement. For instance, the group in the lunchroom that gets the most popsicle sticks in their library pocket gets to choose what four teachers and what song they will perform to on Friday.

Here's another example: If the red team wins today, they get to choose what 5 questions I give the answers to- if the green team wins today they get to choose what 5 questions I give the answers to. Surprisingly, they will work for it.

### — Ignoring
http://tinyurl.com/ignorethemandtheywillgoaway

For **minor disruptions** in the classroom. Ignoring minor behaviors actually teaches the student they cannot get attention by having those behaviors and they will go away. This works if the function of the behavior is teacher attention. The minute the student is doing something right- give them tons of attention. The minute they engage in inappropriate behavior go back to ignoring. The longer you have been giving the behavior air time- the longer it will take the ignoring to work.

### — Love Notes
http://tinyurl.com/lovenotes4kids

For **minor disruptions in the classroom**- this works well. Every single day, every single student went home with a love note. Every night I would take a stack of post-it notes and write:

> Dear student's name,
>
> I love the way you:
>
>
> Love,
>
> Miss Riffel

Each student had one. I would watch the students and write down something positive about them that happened that day:
"I love the way you picked up Sarah's crayon when it rolled off the desk and handed it back to her."
"I love the way you held the door open for me when my arms were full."
"I love the way you walked Billy down to the nurse when he fell and scraped his knee."
In 2006, one of my parents emailed me to find out how I was doing and tell me that her son was graduating. I had been his teacher for three years. She told me a bunch of things and then said, "PS, he still has every single love note you ever gave him."
It really makes a difference to the students.

### — Peer Modeling
http://tinyurl.com/kupeermodels

**To Decrease Horseplay and Disruptions**. Many times this is saved for those students with the best behavior- surprisingly, students who tend to play around – when given peer modeling duties will rise to the occasion and become a great role model. We did this in the third poorest county in the US, where students were more interested in joining gangs than being in the Boy Scouts. We picked the least likely students and they surprised the daylights out of us by being wonderful role models when we showed them we had the faith in them.

### — Proximity
http://tinyurl.com/proximityasteachingtool

**Disruptive Outbursts and just for general classroom management.** Teachers should use proximity and I believe if the room is set up in a semi-circle with the teacher in the middle, the students will all be in close proximity to the teacher. No child should be more than a step or two away from the students.

### — Secret Signals
http://tinyurl.com/secretsignals4teachers

**Minor disruptive behaviors.** Instead of calling students down for inappropriate behavior, keep them after for a few minutes or eat lunch with them and teach them a secret signal that means "cut it out". If you don't embarrass them in front of their peers many times they will stop the behavior. Tugging on your ear, two taps of the chair leg etc.

### — Student/Teacher Rating Sheet
You can download this on www.behaviordoctor.org under materials download.

**Works well for many behaviors you wish to target.** This has been my most popular tool. I think it works better than the ones where the teacher just gives a student a grade for their behavior because the student just thinks, "My teacher gave me a '2'- not I earned a "2". I also believe in using 3-2-1 and not 2-1-0. I don't believe we should give students a 0 to talk about their behavior. They begin to believe they are a zero and that's the way they act.

# Homework Issues

### — Flipped Classroom
http://tinyurl.com/flipoveryourclass

For **students who won't do homework**. I actually don't believe in homework and have studied why it's not the right thing- however, if you must do homework, I would like to see you doing the flipped classroom. The video on the left shows you how it is done.

By Alfie Kohn:

There is no evidence to demonstrate that homework benefits students below high school age. Even if you regard standardized test results as a useful measure (which I don't), more homework *isn't correlated* with higher scores for children in elementary school. The only effect that does show up is less positive attitudes on the part of kids who get more assignments.

• In high school, some studies do find a relationship between homework and test scores, but it tends to be small. More important, there's no reason to think that higher achievement is *caused* by the homework.

• No study has ever confirmed the widely accepted assumption that homework yields *non*academic benefits—self-discipline, independence, perseverance, or better time-management skills—for students of any age. The idea that homework builds character or improves study skills is basically a myth.

### — Homeworkopoly
http://tinyurl.com/templatehomeworkopoly

If you believe in homework and have students who **do not comply by completing their homework** here is a game you can play in your classroom. A lady made this game board and all the pieces and cards that you can download for free. It is a group contingency-group reinforcement for the classroom.

# Impulsiveness

## — Fidget Tools
http://tinyurl.com/fidgets4all

> For students with **impulse control issues, sensory needs, or inattentiveness**. Fidgeting increases retention by 39%.
> - National Institute of Health, 2013
> - Roland Rotz, Ph.D., Sarah D. Wright
>
> "Doing two things at once, it turns out, can actually help students focus on a primary task."
> - The task should engage a sense other than what is required for the primary task- (listening to music, rubbing Velcro, holding a koosh ball etc.)
>
> These secondary tasks are called fidgets — mindless activities kids can do while working on the primary task.
> Soft
> Quiet
> One handed
> Tool not toy

## — Loss of Choice at Recess- Never Take Away Recess
http://tinyurl.com/recessisgood4you

> Students who misbehave typically have **impulsive behaviors**. Many teachers at the elementary level, take away their recess. When you take away a child's recess you punish yourself. Besides, the students spend their whole recess mad at you. We want them to suffer the consequences of their behavior- not plot retaliation. I took away choice at recess. I always knew exactly what they liked to play at recess. I would say, "I'm so sorry you chose to have that behavior. Because of this you lose your choice at recess. You can play everything except soccer." The child will spend their whole recess mad at themselves trying to figure out what to play during recess. I never had to do it twice.

## — Messenger
http://tinyurl.com/studenterrandrunner

> For **students who have a lot of extra energy**. When you see the 13th Mentos teetering on the top of the diet coke, send them to the Library with a Library book to return, take a message to the office (even if it's a fake number with the smiley face). (Make sure the person on the other end knows the secret code. If you get a number with a smiley face- say thank you and send the student back.) Save this for the 13th Mentos and not the 1-12th because if the student figures out that being antsy gets them a trip down the hall- they will show antsy all the time.

# Inattentiveness

### --Class Secretary

For students who have **inattentiveness**. Sometimes I like to whisper to a student that I need to keep myself facing forward. Would they mind being the one to run the smartboard (don't worry- I'll tell you what to press) or write on the board for me (don't worry I'll tell you what to write). This keeps the students busy and on task and helps the student pay attention. It's not a punishment- kind of a privilege- but helps the student at the same time.

### — Vibrating Watch
http://www.eseasongear.com/viviwa.html

Originally used for potty training. Discovered it works well for students with **ADHD to remind them to pay attention**. I also use it as a reminder to catch kids being good.

# Memory

## — Memory Testing
http://faculty.washington.edu/chudler/chmemory.html

To work on **memory skills** before testing. Bring in 20 items and give the students three minutes to look at it. Then cover it with a sheet. Ask the students to write down as many things they remember. Each day change the items and have the students work on their memory skills.

# Negativity

— **Jen Ratio** (3x5 card, beads on lanyard, bracelet, paperclips in pockets)
http://tinyurl.com/jenratio

For students who are **negative, make negative comments, or are engaging in minor non-compliance**. Jen ratio is actually counting the number of positives (numerator) to the number of negatives (denominator). The number of positives should outweigh the negatives by 4 to 1 at least. Eventually, move your Jen Ratio to 8 to 1.

Get a 3x5 card and put the date on it. Make tears on the long side every time you give a positive compliment and tears on the short side every time you get after the students. At the end of the day figure up how many positives to how many negatives you have.

# Negative Self-Talk

— Affirmations
http://www.creativeaffirmations.com/positive-affirmations-for-kids.html

For students with **negative self-talk**. Write ten affirmations on the board each day and give students 2 or 3 post-it notes. Have them choose 2 or 3 per day to take home and put on their mirror.

I do not own the rights to this picture. Taken from google images.

# Non-Compliance

— **Equal Choices**
http://tinyurl.com/equalmotivation

>For students who are **non-compliant**. The National Education Association, and many other researchers have found that offering equal choices keeps students in frontal cortex. A student is more likely to comply if offered equal choices rather than a threat. Instead of saying, "Do this or lose your recess"- a teacher should have two math papers- they can even be the same 20 problems (just in a different order). Walk over to the student's desk and say, "You can do this math paper or this math paper. It doesn't matter to me which you choose. Can't wait to see which one you do." The teacher walks away and uses expected compliance and the student over 90% of the time will choose one and begin.

— **Hairy Eyeball**
http://tinyurl.com/hairyeyeballs

>For **minor disruptions and non-compliance**. The problem with this one is some teachers don't realize who they can do it with and who they should not use this with. Some students when they see the hairy eyeball will straighten right up and others when viewing the hairy eyeball turn into "those are fighting words and we are going to the mat". We need to keep in mind which students this works for and which they don't.

— **Right Ear**
http://tinyurl.com/rightearresearch

>**For Non-Compliance**. Offering equal choices in the right ear or on the right side of student will net great results. The right ear is connected to the left side of the brain. This is where language is processed and the student is more likely to comply when the information is offered on the right ear.

— **Teacher Helper**
http://tips.atozteacherstuff.com/237/classroom-jobs/

>**For off task behavior, non-compliance, or students who need proprioceptive input**. Teacher helper is a great tool to keep students engaged and on task.

# Off Task Behavior

## — Whole Brain Teaching
Www.wholebrainteaching.com

**To increase on task behavior and student engagement.** I just love Chris Biffle's Whole Brain Teaching. It's a way to engage all the students, no student is off task, and topics are taught in small chunks.

# Personal Space Issues

## Hula Hoop
http://tinyurl.com/personalspacecampbook

For **students who do not understand personal space**. I like to use hula-hoops to teach them about personal space. The smaller ones from the dollar store are best. There is also a great book called "Personal Space Camp".

# Reinforcing Replacement Behavior

- **Satiation – Why Reinforcements Don't Work Forever**
  http://tinyurl.com/satiationnmaterialrewards

**About Reinforcements.** Some schools and teachers use the same Reinforcements all year. I like cherry pie, but if I ate it every day- eventually, I wouldn't like it any longer. On Behavior Doctor's website, there are 32 pages of free Reinforcements on the material download page. It's easy to change up the reinforcers.

# Replacement Behaviors

## Video Modeling

http://tinyurl.com/videomodeling4students

http://tinyurl.com/schoolbasedvideomodeling

**Works for many different behaviors. Classroom Management Strategy.** Tons of research on how effective video modeling is on changing behavior. You can find tons of great models on www.pbisvideos.com

## Video Self-Modeling

http://www.siskin.org/www/docs/12/

**To teach new behaviors.** Video self-modeling has been in the research for a long time- but it has been very popular since 2003. Almost every journal has at least one article about it. This is done by using the student as the main actor. Only the appropriate behavior is shown and labeled.

# Self-Esteem (Lack of)

── **Class Helper**
http://tinyurl.com/K8classhelper   (K-8)  For **self-esteem issues, impulsiveness, disruptions**.

Giving the student a job to do in the classroom can alleviate a bevy of behavioral woes. When students have low self-esteem, a class job can help them feel good about themselves. For students who are impulsive, the proprioceptive input they get from getting up and performing a task can help them concentrate. Rerouting disruptions into an actual job in the classroom (like announcing the page numbers) can keep students who burp and blurt on track.

── **Class Meetings**
http://tinyurl.com/classmeetings2

For **self-esteem, disruptions, non-compliance, and other issues that arise**. I first learned about classroom meetings from Vanderbilt University and found them to be extremely advantageous. There are great ways to incorporate core curriculum into the morning meetings. You can also infuse classroom review of rules, compliments, turn taking, handling problems in a pro-social way.  Here is the structure of my morning meeting:

- Compliments (each person gets 1 compliment) I start. I use a koosh ball. I compliment someone. That person gets the koosh ball and they compliment someone else and the koosh ball gets tossed to that person. It makes all the kids pay attention to what is being said because they never know who will be left when they get the koosh ball.  They pay attention to each other so they can think of something to say. I also taught them what a compliment was- it is not something you see on the outside like shoes, haircut etc. It is something inside like kindness, politeness, patience- etc.
- Then we handled what we were going to be doing that day – like an auditory and visual schedule for the whole class.
- Then we handled any issues which had arisen in the problem box.  I did not use names- I would just say, "It has been brought to my attention that there is a problem on the playground with "xyz" and not using names I would describe the problem.  The students would vote on how they were going to handle it and then they would all agree that was how they would handle the situation in the future.
- We would check-in on previous issues and see how they were going.
- We would end with a celebration of success from the day before.
    - The day would start.

── **Each One Save Five**
http://tinyurl.com/mentoringinschool

For students with **low self-esteem**, students with any behavioral or academic concerns, **basically all the students** in the school should be part of this. Take the total number of students in the school divided by the total number of adults in the building (this is counting secretaries, custodians, cafeteria workers). That is your number. Each adult must make contact with their 5-9 students (those are the averages I've found) once a week through:

- Email to parent
- Phone message on answering machine
- Letter in their locker or desk
- Note delivered to first hour class
- Post card mailed home
- Positive phone call home
- High five in the hallway

## --Finding the Gift of Every Disability (No Excuses)
http://tinyurl.com/giftofadhd
http://www.dyslexia.com/
http://thegiftsofautism.com/
http://tinyurl.com/encouragingodd

> For **self-esteem** issues. Sometimes when students have behaviors they will say, "I can't help it. I have ADHD, Autism etc." I always say- every disability comes with a gift. Let's figure out how to use your gifts. The books above are a great start for you.

## —— Four P's for Raising Self-Esteem (Power, Proficiency, Public Relations, Philanthropy)
http://www.behaviordoctor.org/files/tools/4-Ps%20Worksheet.pdf

> For students with **low self-esteem**. When children are 6 years old, 80% of them have high self-esteem. When children are 10 years old 20% of them have high self-esteem. By the time those same children get to high school only 5% of them have high self-esteem (Campbell, 2009). The four P's are:
>
> - Public Relations- how can we make this child look good in front of their peers.
> - Proficiency- what skills are they lacking academically and behaviorally?
> - Power- what can we teach the student to do to have power over their emotions?
>   - Philanthropy- it's very hard to feel bad about yourself when you are helping someone else.

## --Philanthropy
www.freerice.com

http://www.prweb.com/releases/2010/02/prweb3657524.htm

> **To raise self-esteem**. It's really hard to feel bad about yourself when you are helping someone else. This can be done through peer tutoring, peer modeling etc.- but you can also let them be in charge of philanthropy efforts (counting can and box donations for the food pantry) announcing over the intercom how many pounds of donations have been brought in to the school etc. You can also let them play on www.freerice.com and earn free rice for a third world country.

# Sensory Input

## — Proprioceptive Input
http://sensorysmarts.com/sensory_diet_activities.html

> For students who need **sensory input**. We all need this. Activities that let us know where our body is in time and space. As adults, we have figured out socially appropriate ways to do this- twiddling our foot up and down, shifting in our seat and so on. We need to help students figure out how to engage in this – it helps them pay attention. Padding their chairs, putting therapy banding between the two front chair legs and teaching the students how to bounce their feet up and down on the banding, how to shift in their seats will help keep them seated and paying attention.

## — Seating Choices
http://tinyurl.com/wobblechair

http://tinyurl.com/balancedisks

> There should be some kind of cushion on the chair. Especially little boys whose tailbones have no pocket of fat between their tailbone and the hard surface we are asking them to sit on. This is also true for the students with **ADHD, Sensory Integration Disorder, and/or Autism**.

## — Sensory Break
http://tinyurl.com/sensorybreaks

> **Need for sensory input**- We all need breaks and sometimes the classroom becomes so focused on meeting core curriculum, we forget to give kids a brain break. If we have just taught them a huge chunk of information, we need to let that digest by giving them a sensory break- this is for the neurotypical students. The students with autism or sensory integration disorder need sensory breaks more frequently. The occupational therapist in the district can help you determine which sensory break is appropriate for each student.

## — Sensory Diet
http://sensorysmarts.com/sensory_diet_activities.html

> **Sensory Input**. This has nothing to do with eating ☺ A sensory diet is a schedule that builds in the sensory breaks prior to each activity. It is based on what the student needs prior to each upcoming activity.

# Sleepiness in Class

## Drinking Water
http://tinyurl.com/waterboostsgrades

For **sleepy** students. Drinking water in school-

- Students should be encouraged to carry water bottles
- Water hydrates the brain
    - Students who drink water:
        - improved their scores by up to 10%
        - performed an average of 5% better than students who did not drink any water.
            - It's been law since 2010 that schools provide to students more frequently.

## Eight Hours of Sleep
http://tinyurl.com/kidsneedsleep8

For students who are consistently **tired**: Share the following with parents:

- Here are some guidelines:
    - 1-3 years old– 13-14 hrs a day
    - 3-6 years old– 10.5-12 hrs a day
    - 7-12 — 10-11 hrs a day
    - 13-18– 8 ¼ -9 ½ hrs a day
- These are from WebMD- Ask parents to do the math and backtrack from the time they have to get their children up in the morning.
    - Getting enough sleep decreases cortisol in your blood
    - Behavior problems are linked to cortisol levels

— http://www.sciencedaily.com/releases/2011/02/110209124143.htm

## Spritzing the Room
http://www.starchaser-healingarts.com/product/energetic-spritz-hyrdrosol-based/
http://tinyurl.com/calmingspritzer

**Revving up or slowing down the internal engines.** We can change the mood of the room by spritzing before the students come in (don't do this with the students in the room). Peppermint extract mixed in the water will wake the students up. Lavender oil mixed with the water will calm the students down.

# Social Skills Deficit

— **Lunch Bunch**
   http://tinyurl.com/lunchbunchsocialskills

   For **social skills, counseling (private), teaching of secret signals, and discussing behaviors in private**- invite one student at a time or a small group with same issues to eat lunch with you. You can also use this to help build friendship skills for students with low social skills.

— **Social Skills Training**
   http://www.socialskilltrainingproject.com/

   For **children who have few social skills**. When I taught Kindergarten back in the 1980's the core curriculum in Kindergarten was teaching social skills. People ask me now why kids have worse behavior. I don't actually think kids are worse now than they used to be- but we have condensed the curriculum down so far that we teach reading and math skills in kindergarten now instead of social skills. We have to start teaching social skills mixed in with our curriculum if we want students to know how to work peacefully etc.

**-Social Instructional Groups (just like Academic Instructional Groups)**

   Pull out lessons
   - Second Step Lessons run by paraprofessionals (video program with worksheets)
     - http://www.cfchildren.org/second-step
     - early years through 8th grade
     - randomized control trials - http://www.cfchildren.org/second-step/research
   - Who can conduct:
     - Principal Flex Time
     - Counselor Groups
       - Lunch Bunch
   - How it can be delivered:
     - Pre-written modules
     - Video Models
     - Video Self-Modeling
     - Social Autopsies

# Stress

## — Feng Shui Research
http://tinyurl.com/funkswayinclass

If the classroom seems **stressed** as a whole. The book link to the left is a great book that describes how to use Feng Shui in the classroom. This is a very researched science and is used by big businesses to increase productivity. It is worth checking out for the classroom.

## — Lights
www.huelight.net

Do fluorescent lights trigger migraines?

http://well.blogs.nytimes.com/2010/09/02/do-fluorescent-lights-trigger-migraines/?_php=true&_type=blogs&_r=0 –

Do fluorescent lights cause stress? (hence behavior)

http://skeptics.stackexchange.com/questions/7510/do-fluorescent-lights-cause-stress

For students who are **impulsive, have sensory overload, or attention deficit hyperactivity disorder**.

The huelight panels have been known to decrease stress related behaviors. The hypothesis is that eye strain might cause these behaviors. Here's an excerpt from a principal who has them in every light in her school.

"I have spoken directly to a parent who had a child with vision problems (convergence disorder) and she shared what the panels did for her child was eliminate the need for color overlays which he had had to use to help him with classroom work. He noticed immediately his ability to read the words on the page without these aides. He also reported fewer headaches as a result of the panels being installed.

Teachers report the lighting in the classroom with the Huelight panels sets the tone for a quieter, calmer learning environment. Overall in the building, our behavior referrals continue to decrease. We feel we owe much of this to the positive behavior intervention supports we've put in place and the addition of the Huelight panels."

Kim Rampey- principal- Jefferson Elementary – Union Public Schools

# Talking

## Voice Level- using ruler

**For loud talkers.** I use a ruler to teach students how loud to talk. A zero-inch voice means no talking- my ear could be next to their lips and I wouldn't hear anything. A three-inch voice means the student would be whispering. A six-inch voice is a soft voice and so on.

# Tantrum

## — Clear the Room- Remove the Audience
http://tinyurl.com/removeaudience

When a student is having a **tantrum** and furniture is flying- I have witnessed adults getting hurt trying to transport the student down to the office. It is better to take the rest of the class down to the library with their work and to deal with the student tantrum in the classroom. Transporting a child can hurt the child or the adults. Once you get the student calm, the student can walk with you to the office to work on a social autopsy to help them figure out how to avoid this in the future.

## — First/Then (Now/Then)
http://tinyurl.com/firstthenvisualschedule

For students who throw **tantrums** because they want a preferred activity rather than a non-preferred activity. This is a simplified visual schedule.

I do not own the rights to these pictures. They are from Pinterest.

## — Screening (Decreasing Peer Attention)
http://www.positiveparentingsolutions.com/parenting/public-tantrums

When a student drops on the floor and has a **tantrum**- every adult that walks by will ask them to get up (tons of adult attention) and every student that walks by will give them attention. Put up a blue padded mat from the PE room so no one can see the student who has dropped on the floor. This will keep the student from getting attention and should stop the tantrums if the function of the tantrum is to get attention.

## — Visualization Strategies
http://udleditions.cast.org/strategy_visualize.html

**To Decrease Tantrums**. Visualizing the proper behavior, the proper way to work a problem is a valuable technique we need to teach to students. Much like a runner visualizes themselves crossing the finish line, the student visualizes themselves calming down, doing their work, or engaging in appropriate behavior.

# Tardies

- **Rolling Alarm Clock (Clocky)**
  http://tinyurl.com/clockytardies

  **For students who are habitually tardy.** This is a great clock that when you set the alarm, it rolls off the table and rolls around the room when the alarm goes off. The student has to get up to turn it off. It helps them being on time to school.

# Transition Difficulties

## --Vanna White

When you have a student who has a **hard time transitioning**, put them in charge of the transition for the whole class. Make them Vanna White of the daily schedule.

## — Visual Schedule

http://tinyurl.com/visualschedules4class

**For students who have trouble with transitions**. We all like to cross off "to do" lists. Our students with special needs actually thrive well on this. The link on the left has great samples of visual schedules.

# References

Achenbach, T. M. (1991). *Manual for child behavior checklist.* Burlington, VT: University of Vermont, Dept. of Psychiatry.

Alberto, P., & Troutman, A. (2003). *Applied behavior analysis for teachers* (6th ed.). Upper Saddle River, NJ: Merrill Prentice-Hall.

Alliance for Excellent Education. (n.d.). *About the crisis.* Retrieved August 21, 2010, from http://www.all4ed.org/about_the_crisis

Atchison, B. (2007). *Sensory modulation disorders among children with a history of trauma: a frame of reference.* Kalamazoo, WI. Language Speech and Hearing (April 38, (2) 109-116.

Bambara, L., Dunlap, G., & Schwartz, I. (2004). *Positive behavior support: Critical articles on improving practice for individuals with severe disabilities.* Dallas, Texas: Pro-Ed.

Bambara, L. M., & Knoster, T. (1998). Designing positive behavior support plans. Innovations – Research to Practice Series. Washington, DC. American Association on Mental Retardation.

Bandura, A. (1976). Effecting change through participant modeling principles. In J. D. Krumboltz & C. E. Thorensen (Eds.), *Self-control: Power to the person* (pp. 86–110). Pacific Grove, CA: Brooks/Cole.

Bhaerman, R., & Kopp, K. (1988). *The school's choice: Guidelines for dropout prevention at the middle and junior high school.* Columbus, Ohio: Naitonal Center of Research in Vocational Education.

Blanchard, K., & Lorber, R. (1984). Putting the one-minute manager to work: How to turn the 3 secrets into skills. New York, NY: Berkley.

Brandmeir, J. (Director). (2006). *The child connection* [Motion Picture]. USA: Better Life Media.

Brown, F., Gothelf, C., Guess, D., & Lehr, D. (2004). Self-determination for individuals with the most severe disabilities: Moving beyond chimera. In L. Bambara, G. Dunlap, & I.

Schwartz, *Positive behavior support: Critical articles on improving practice for individuals with severe disabilities* (pp. 22–31). Dallas, Texas: Pro-Ed.

Burke, M., Davis, J., Lee, Y. H., & Hagan-Burke, S. (in press). Universal screening for behavioral risk in elementary schools using SWPBS expectations. *Journal of Emotional Behavior Disorders*

Center for Disease Control and Prevention. (2010, November 12). *Morbinity and mortality weekly report.* Retrieved February 14, 2011, from http://www.cdc.gov/mmwr/pdf/wk/mm5944.pdf.

Crisis. (n.d.). In *WordNet* web. Retrieved from http://wordnetweb.princeton.edu/perl/webwn?s=crisis.

Crone, D., & Horner, R. (2003). *Building positive behavior support systems in schools.* New York, NY: Guilford Press.

Data Accountability Center. (2008). *Welcome to Data Accountability Center.* Retrieved August 21, 2010, from https://www.ideadata.org.

Drummond, T. (1993). *The student risk screening scale (SRSS).* Grants Pass, OR: Josephine County Mental Health Program.

DuFour, R., Eaker, R., Karhanek, G., & DuFour, R. (2004). *Whatever it takes: How professional learning communities respond when kids don't learn.* Bloomington, IN: Solution Tree.

Durand, V. M., & Crimmins, D. B. (1992). *The motivation assessment scale (MAS) administration guide.* Topeka, KS: Monaco and Associates.

Dunlap, G., Iovannone, R., Kincaid, D., Wilson, K., Christiansen, K., Strain, P., et al. (2010). *Prevent teach reinforce.* Baltimore, MA: Brookes.

DuPaul, G., & Weyandt, L. (2006). School-based intervention for children with attention deficit hyperactivity disorder: Effects on academic, social, and behavioural functioning. *International Journal of Disability,* 161–176.

Gelfand, J. L. (2009). *Parenting guide.* Retrieved February 14, 2011, from WebMD, http://www.webmd.com/parenting/guide/sleep-children.

Gresham & Elliott (1990). *Social skills rating system.* Circle Pines, MN: American Guidance Service.

Haydon, T., Conroy, M., Sindelar, P., Scott, T. M., Brian, & Marie, A. (2010). Comparison of Three Types of Opportunities to Respond on Student Academic and Social Behaviors, Journal of Emotional and Behavioral.

Disorders, 18(1), 27-40. Iwata, B., & DeLeon, I. G. (1996). *The functional analysis screening tool.* Gainesville, FL: The Florida Center on Self-Injury.

Kamphaus, R. W., & Reynolds, C. R. (2007). *BASC-2 behavioral and emotional screening system manual.* Circle Pines, MN: Pearson.

Lewis, T. J., Scott, T. M., & Sugai, G. (1994). The problem behavior questionnaire: A teacher-based instrument to develop functional hypotheses of problem behavior in general education settings. *Diagnostique, 19,* 103–115

Live Science (2009). *Want a favor? Whisper in the right ear.* Commission of European Communities.

Marzano, R. (2003). *Classroom management that works: Research-based strategies for every teacher.* Alexandria, VA: Association for Supervision and Curriculum Development.

O'Neill, R., Horner, R., Albin, R., Sprague, J., Storey, K., & Newton, J. (1997). *Functional assessment and program development for problem behavior: A practical handbook* (2nd ed.). Pacific Grove, CA: Brooks.

Parker, H. (2002). *Problem solver guide for students with ADHD*. Plantation, FL: Specialty Press.

Putnam, R. D. (2000). Bowling alone: The collapse and revival of American community. New York, NY: Simon & Schuster.

Putnam, S. (2002). Keeping up the motivation to exercise. *CHADD: ATTENTION*, 21–25

Rief, S. (2005). *How to reach and teach children with ADD/ADHD*. San Francisco, CA: Jossey-Bass.

Walker, H. M., Severson, H. H. (1992). *Systematic screening for behavior disorders*. Longmont, CO: Sopris West.

Sheets, S. (2008). *Apnea*. Retrieved February 14, 2011, from Kids Health, http://kidshealth.org/parent/general/sleep/apnea.html.

Sheridan, S. (1995). *The tough kid social skills book*. Longmont, CO: Sopris West.

Shores, R., Gunter, P., & Jack, S. (1993). Classroom management strategies: Are they setting events for coercion? *Behavioral Disorders*, 92–102

Springer Science Business Media. (2009, June 23). Need something? Talk to my right ear. *Science Daily*. Retrieved February 14, 2011, from http://www.sciencedaily.com/releases/2009/06/090623090705.html.

Towers, R. L. (1987). *How schools can help combat student drug and alcohol abuse*. Washington, DC: National Education Association of the United States.

U.S. Department of Education. (1986). *Schools without drugs*. Washington, DC: Author.

Webb, J. (2000). Mis-diagnosis and dual diagnosis of gifted children: Gifted and LD, ADHD, OCD, oppositional defiant disorder. *Annual Conference of the American Psychological Association* (p. 15). Washington DC: N/A

Whitaker, B. (2010, May 28). *CBS reports*. Retrieved August 21, 2010, from CBS News: http://www.cbsnews.com/stories/2010/05/28/eveningnews/main6528227.shtml?tag=currentVideoInfo;videoMetaInfo.

Made in the USA
Columbia, SC
02 March 2020